Anastasia Dolby

Church Vestments

Their Origin, Use and Ornament - Practically Illustrated

Anastasia Dolby

Church Vestments
Their Origin, Use and Ornament - Practically Illustrated

ISBN/EAN: 9783337259013

Printed in Europe, USA, Canada, Australia, Japan

Cover: Foto ©Thomas Meinert / pixelio.de

More available books at **www.hansebooks.com**

CHURCH VESTMENTS:

THEIR

Origin, Use, and Ornament

PRACTICALLY ILLUSTRATED.

BY ANASTASIA DOLBY,
AUTHORESS OF "CHURCH EMBROIDERY, ANCIENT AND MODERN,"
AND
LATE EMBROIDERESS TO THE QUEEN.

LONDON:
CHAPMAN & HALL, 193, PICCADILLY.
1868.

LONDON : PRINTED BY WILLIAM CLOWES AND SONS, STAMFORD STREET
AND CHARING CROSS.

PREFACE.

The favourable reception given to my Work on "Church "Embroidery" has induced me to publish this volume.

The practical directions conveyed in the former book are as applicable to the ornamentation of the priestly dress as they are to the enrichment of the Sanctuary, and are based upon principles of experience, which require to be but once laid down to serve for ever. It may therefore, justly, be supposed, that upon the actual manipulation of Ecclesiastical Needlework I have no longer a cause for writing.

Still, as a vestment-maker, I observe an undoubted demand for special instruction concerning just forms, correct designs, and fitting materials for the robes appointed to be worn by the Ministers of the Catholic Church in the discharge of their holy functions.

The practical knowledge of sacerdotal vesture brought to bear in the following pages may be conscientiously dated from the period when the late A. W. Pugin commenced his laudable raid against the incongruous and undignified array of the Christian priesthood of the past, and first half of the present, century.

At a very early age I became a subscriber to his rules for the revival of true beauty in sacred art, and day by day am more convinced that, in the main, those principles are right.

Preface.

From this admission, an advocacy for the strictly Gothic in Church designs may be inferred. Such is not quite the case, although the supposed prejudice might be well justified in the fact, that the Early Mediæval Period, in which is comprehended the pure Gothic style, was that when symmetrical forms in rich decoration came the nearest in sacred, as in secular, art to human ideas of perfection.

In this, as in my former work, nothing in the way of research has been spared for the elucidation of my subject. Where I have needed liturgical and archæological assistance from living celebrities, I have stood within the boundary of my own province to ask their aid, and in every instance have been kindly and generously enlightened.

My husband has again devoted much valuable time and energy to the illustration of my treatise. We have gone through it together, literally hand in hand, that it might be brought forth in some degree worthily, and with credit to the faith we have striven to honour.

A. D.

Highgate, 1868.

CONTENTS.

I.
INTRODUCTION—Origin, Use, and Ornament of Church Vestments . . . PAGE 1

II.
The Amice—The Alb—The Girdle . . . 26

III.
The Chasuble—Its changes of Form, since its Origin, explained—Various Ways of Ornamenting the Vestment described and Illustrated . . . 43

IV.
Different Materials of which a Chasuble may, and may not, be made—General Directions for making-up Vestments . . . 68

V.
The Dalmatic of the Deacon—Tunicle of the Sub-Deacon . 78

VI.
The Sacrificial Stole—The Maniple—The Stolone—The Confessional Stole—The Baptismal Stole—The Preaching Stole . . . 86

VII.
The Cope—The Hood—The Orphreys—The Morse . . . 101

VIII.
The Offertory Veil—The Chalice Veil—The Burse . 113

Contents.

IX.
The Surplice—The Cotta 121

X.
The Sacred Linen of the Altar—Corporal-Cloths—Palls—Purificators—Lavabor-towels 127

XI.
The Canon's Cope—The Furred Amys . . . 131

XII.
The Mitre—The Rochet—The Subcingulum—The Gremiale—The Cappa Magna—The Mozetta—The Buskins—The Sandals—The Gloves 135

XIII.
The Pallium—The Fanon 167

XIV.
The Cassock—The Biretta—The Roman Collar . . 171

XV.
Proper Colours for the Sacred Vestments . . . 174

XVI.
Embroidery Stitches of the Anglo-Saxon and Early Mediæval Periods—Illustrated by 12 Engraved Examples 177

XVII.
The Vestment-maker's Charge to the Sacristan . . 186

XVIII.
Frontispiece, of Pontifical High Mass, described . . 191

LIST OF ILLUSTRATIONS.

	PAGE
Coloured Frontispiece. . . . . *For Description, see*	191
Group of Ecclesiastics from the Psalter of Richard II. .	1
Three Designs for the Amice	26
Priests in Albs, from Procession of St. Alban's Shrine .	32
Correct Form of Alb	38
Circular Chasuble of the Early Christians . . .	44
Bishops of Ravenna, from Mosaics of the Sixth Century	48
Eadulphus being made first Archbishop of Lichfield .	50
Chasuble of St. Thomas of Canterbury . . .	52
Examples of the Chasuble, from Sculptured Figures of the Middle Ages	56
Vested Priests, from MSS. of the Twelfth and Thirteenth Centuries	58
Ancient Example of the Crucifix upon the Chasuble .	60
Richly Vested Figure of Thomas de la Mare .	62
Back of fine old Chasuble found at Abergavenny .	64
Front of the same	66
Vestment from the Cathedral of Aix-la-Chapelle .	68
Example of an *Incorrect* Form of the Chasuble	72
Two Designs for the Anglo-Saxon "Flower" .	74
Design of Agnus Dei for the Y Cross . . .	76
Design for the Latin Cross on the Chasuble. . .	78
Chasuble to be used for Services of our Lady . .	80
Ancient Figures of Deacons, and Correct Form of Dalmatic.	82
Deacon and Sub-Deacon, from a Gregorian Sacramentary	84
The Orarium, and Stole, from very old examples .	88
Three Designs for Baptismal and Preaching Stoles .	98

List of Illustrations.

	PAGE
Design for Orphrey of Cope	102
Two Designs for Hoods of Cope	106
Two Designs, suitable either for the Chasuble or the Hood of Cope	114
Practical Illustrations of the Chalice-Veil, and Burse	118
Figure of Thurifer in Surplice, from Matthew Paris	121
True Form of the Surplice	122
Examples of different Vestments, on Figures from Queen Mary's Psalter	124
Acolytes in Surplices, from Queen Mary's Psalter	128
Figure of Canon in Rochet, from Molinet	144
Examples of the Crimped and Crochet Cotta	146
Designs of Crosses for Stoles, and "Gammadion" Stole	152
Borders for Albs	158
Various Ancient Examples of the Mitre, and Sandals	162
The Fanon, Pallium, and Mozetta	170
Examples of Anglo-Saxon and Mediæval Embroidery Stitches	177—185

CHURCH VESTMENTS.

I.
INTRODUCTION.

"And thou shalt make holy
"garments for Aaron thy bro-
"ther for glory and for beauty.
"And thou shalt speak unto
"all that are wise-hearted, whom
"I have filled with the spirit of
"wisdom, that they may make
"Aaron's garments to consecrate
"him, that he may minister unto
"me in the priest's office.
"And these are the garments
"which they shall make; a
"breastplate, and an ephod, and
"a robe, and a broidered coat,
"a mitre, and a girdle."
EXODUS, *ch.* xxviii.,
ver. 2, 3, 4.

THIS emphatic and direct command of God for the apparelling of His ministers, in a manner which should not only distinguish but consecrate them for His service in the Tabernacle, should be precedent enough for any amount of zeal manifested

Church Vestments.

in promoting the enrichment of the sacred garments of the Priesthood, which by the Divine and undeviating Word was established as "a statute for ever."

The ceremonial of the priestly dress so clearly enjoined for the Church of the Law is nowhere abrogated in the Gospel, and if, as true believers, we accept what St. John beheld in his vision of the Church in Heaven, as the type of that which should glorify the worship of the Almighty Father in His Church upon earth, we, who find our vocation in working vestments for the servants of the Lord, should hold ourselves bound to favour no sacerdotal garment, or decoration thereupon, which is not especially produced for, and, as far as piety and human means can qualify it, regally worthy of, the solemn services of the King of Kings.

It would be as presumptuous as futile to attempt to say or suggest anything original on correct Sacerdotal Vesture.

Were we aught else greater than needleworkers, we could not take upon ourselves to teach the present generation how to make exterior things, appertaining to the worship of the true God, grander, more solemn, and more worthy of the Divine Majesty, than the inspired early followers of the faith made them.

We all know that from the first Christian days especial garments were set apart for the sacred rites of the Altar, and that for some time they continued to be worn secular in shape and ornamentation, principally that the observation of heathen persecutors might be avoided. The forms which now distinguish the robes of the Roman priesthood must of necessity have had their origin in the ordinary dress of the people among whom the primitive Christians lived and walked; but we have no difficulty in believing that, after such garments had been once consecrated to the service of the Holy Eucharist, they were kept exclusive

Their Origin, Use, and Ornament.

for the like sacred usage. Equally sure may we be that the vicissitudes of fashion, whatever they may have done in transforming the costume of the laity, were allowed to have no material effect on that of the sacerdotal community. Every good authority which we can bring to bear upon the subject agrees in assuring us that the main features of Ecclesiastical dress have remained unaltered from the first, and, with few exceptions, as we recognise them in the Roman Catholic Church of the present day. Before proceeding further, we would observe, that after comparing all the gleanings we have made in ancient sacerdotal lore from different popular sources with the writings of Dr. Daniel Rock, we are bound to admit that we can say nothing relevant to our subject, and historically correct, that he has not already said in one or other of his works, which literally embody, in a terse and truthful form, every interesting chronicle of every reliable authority that has gone before.

If therefore, during the progress of our work, we may lay ourselves open to the charge of slavishness by quoting precedents more freely from the learned divine we have cited than from any other archæological historian, we must claim to shield ourselves by our plea of conscientiousness alone.

From the end of the sixth century may be dated the exclusive adoption by the Church, of robes identical in form with those ordinarily worn by people of condition in Rome in the infant days of Christianity. Still, long prior to the above, we gather much from the historian Anastasius respecting the beauty and costliness of the Holy Vestments, from the Emperor Aurelian, A.D. 275, downwards to the period when the great Constantine enrolled himself beneath the Christian banner, and the ministering servants of the Holy Altar, emboldened by his zeal and upheld by his power, enriched in every possible way the sacred garments of their office, the greater to honour and glorify the Lord of All.

According to Dr. Rock, the glory of the sacred ritual which shone forth after the conversion of the Emperor Constantine must have been sublime as it was dazzling. We quote from "Hierurgia:"—

"From the moment that Constantine declared himself a "Christian, the ceremonies of religion were performed with "splendour, and regal magnificence shone throughout the "sacred ritual. Before this period, the garments of the priest- "hood at the altar, though not always, were more frequently "composed of the less expensive materials, and decorated merely "with a scarlet stripe, which was then denominated 'Latus- "clavus.' This was now exchanged for a vesture, the same "indeed in form, but manufactured of the richest stuffs.

"The sacred habit presented by Constantine to Macarius, the "bishop of Jerusalem, to be employed by that prelate in admi- "nistering the sacrament of baptism, was made of cloth of gold, "as we gather from the testimony of Theodoretus."—*Hist.* lib. ii. c. 22.

It was now, too, that the strips of cloth called "clavi," which hitherto had been used for ornamenting the priestly dress, in accordance with its secular type, began to be exchanged for bands of costlier material—orphreys—to correspond with the greater splendour of the fabric of the robe.

Here we must pause to remark upon a peculiarity with reference to the colour of those bands denominated "clavi," which distinguished, in the way of ornament, the dresses of the Roman people before, and long after, the coming of the Saviour. We speak of the so-called *purple*—under which denomination came blood-red, crimson, scarlet, and, without doubt, the shade we now

Their Origin, Use, and Ornament.

designate as rose-purple. A very interesting record relating to the ancient imperial purple is embodied thus :—Three hundred and thirty-one years before Christ, Alexander possessing himself of the city of Susa, with all its riches, took from it five thousand quintals of the highly-prized Hermione purple, which, although stored there for one hundred and ninety years, was without a blemish when it fell into the conqueror's hands. The value of this wonderful colour was equivalent to one hundred crowns a pound; and, as a quintal was 112 lbs., we may estimate the amount of wealth contained in this dye alone, as something scarcely short of the fabulous.

Among the ancients, we find Greeks, as well as Romans, holding the Tyrian purple in like esteem. Homer fails not to tell us that Andromache wrought in her lofty chamber on a cloth of resplendent purple hue at the moment when mournful cries apprised her of the death of Hector. And the Roman Tarquin received from the Etruscans a purple tunic enriched with gold, and a mantle of purple and other colours.

"It was a custom," says Dr. Rock, "which universally pre-
"vailed amongst the ancient Romans, to ornament every gar-
"ment with stripes of cloth and fringes of a purple colour. The
"stripes were called 'Latus-clavus' if broad, and 'Augustus-
"clavus' if narrow. The breadth of this ornament was com-
"mensurate with the rank and dignity of the wearer."

Anastasius enlightens us as to the splendour of the Church in Rome from the most remote times to the ninth century; but beyond this, for faithful and impartial records of the fitting magnificence of sacred vesture during the early and pure-minded days of Christianity, we may all, whether or not we are interested in the present vexed question of Ritualism, be grateful to Dugdale. That voluminous chronicler, in his "Monasticon," carries

Church Vestments.

us on through the Church in our own land to that epoch—the middle of the sixteenth century, when the glory of the Lord, and honour to His name, were sacrificed to the ambition and avarice of men; and priests and people, whether of just or of erring lives, were alike, only to be tolerated, when seen farthest away from the true worship of their fathers.

The coldest Puritan might shudder, as he follows the chronicler, at the thought of the manner in which we all know thousands of those precious garments consecrated to the service of the Almighty, and fragrant with the incense offered to His throne, were either destroyed, or, what was worse, desecrated by the secular and debased uses to which they were put.

These are truths which should be palpable to all. The records we have searched are accessible to all; and they who read them may perhaps find their store of knowledge profitably increased on many things, which may be of greater importance to some minds than the revival of a taste for sacred needlework. As for ourselves, we have already intimated in our former book that our love for Church Embroidery is greater than our ability or desire for disputation.

We hold our subject in such respect as to deem it fully worthy of more than the life's study we have hitherto made it, and are too grateful to be able to handle it without the necessity for moving one step beyond our womanly province.

It is impossible to close our eyes to the fact that purity of taste in Ecclesiastical ornament was in its decadence long before Henry the Eighth came to the throne. Evidences of the sacrifice of the pious spirit which breathed through the sacred designs of previous times, to secular sentiment and worldly display, are visible prior to the close of the fifteenth century. Up to the time of Henry the Sixth, religious art may be said to have

Their Origin, Use, and Ornament.

advanced, with the age, in beauty and pious sentiment, till it had attained a point of grandeur and exclusive excellence in the representation and construction of sacred objects, from which no step but one of retrogression could well be taken.

During this golden age of artistic merit, the cathedrals of York, Westminster, Durham, and many others, were added to, and embellished with a dazzling splendour, which no amount of wealth, unaided by the pious motive power that originated these wondrous structures, could ever again restore.

The Percy shrine at Beverley, that peerless work of sacred art, was raised under the inspiration of those days; and, battered and mutilated as it has been, is still worthy of a pilgrimage from far-off lands to see.

When we call to mind how Oliver Cromwell did his best to destroy and utterly annihilate every beauteous thing belonging to the ancient Church, which had escaped the covetous eye of Henry the Eighth, the wonder is, that so much has been left to wonder at.

Let us give honour where honour is due. In nearly every corner throughout our land there still exists some touching fragment of a tale told in stone long ages ago, which few of us might read unassisted by those keys, both of the pen and pencil, which the toilers who have gone before laboured so assiduously to leave to us ere the ravages of time should complete the work of obliteration, so cruelly commenced by man, on those nobly sculptured pages.

In like manner do those glorious manuscripts and chronicles enable us to trace with accuracy, and to our edification, the pious origin and history of many a venerable monument in hallowed needlework, which we find faded, transformed, and often misappropriated.

Church Vestments.

Therefore, honoured alike be the memory of historian and artist, who, in spite of a wicked king's avarice and a misguided Puritan's destroying hand, have secured to us yet records enough of art in the true religion of the past to educate our eyes, and enlarge our minds beyond the presumptuous belief that whitewashed walls and robeless priests do well enough for the worship of the Creator, while His creatures raise for themselves luxurious palaces, and adorned in costly garments and priceless jewels, are content to live only in their own glorification. Too often " from "this want of faith in things of God's appointment, are we only "capable of receiving such as please our ears, through some idol "man." And not unfrequently lacking charity, in every Christian phase, even to the bestowal of the cup of cold water in His name.

As, after the so-called Reformation, everything which could remind the people of the grand old Ritual of the past was sedulously swept away, it is not remarkable that those of the present day, who advocate the restoration of the Sacerdotal Vesture of the early and incorrupt Church, should desire to take their precedents from a period long anterior to the "second year of King Edward the Sixth."

In the Anglo-Saxon manuscripts we find beautifully illuminated drawings of sacerdotal costume of a very early date in England; but little is to be discovered in writing respecting the just *forms* of the sacred vestments prior to the Norman Conquest; although, long before then, frequent mention is made of costly gifts to different churches, including chasubles, copes, stoles, albs, and the like.

As, for instance, King Ina, A.D. 708, who rebuilt Glastonbury Abbey, loaded it with sumptuous sacred things.

Dugdale tells us :—" The old abbey church, which he had " new built, he caused to be re-consecrated, and dedicated it to

Their Origin, Use, and Ornament.

"God, in honour of Christ, and the Apostles Peter and Paul. One of the chapels (supposed to be St. Joseph's) he garnished over with gold and silver, and gave to it ornaments and vessels of gold and silver. The gold plate of the gift amounted to 333 lbs. weight, the silver to 2835 lbs. weight, besides the gold and precious gems embroidered in the *celebrating vestments*, according to the account that Speed gives us of this benefaction; but, according to the relation that Stowe and the English martirologe give of it, it came to a great deal more."

Again, it is recorded of Egelric, elected abbat of Croyland in the year 984, that "He gave numerous vestments to the office of the sacrist, viz.: to every altar in the church two chasubles, one for Sundays, and another richer; to the choir twenty-four copes, six white, six red, six green, and six black;" besides clothing "the whole convent every year with gowns, every second year with hoods, and every third year with frocks, at his own expense."

"The doomed and often suffering,• but always magnificent Croyland Abbey," must have been greatly enriched by vestments. King Canute, on his return from Rome, A.D. 1032, was met at Sandwich by Abbat Brithmer of Croyland, who presented him with two palfreys, upon which the king gave the abbat a vestment of silk, interwoven with eagles of gold.

Meet cause must it have been for gratulation when, upon the destruction of the abbey by fire in 1091, the contents of the sacred wardrobe, owing to the double stone roof of the vestry, were found uninjured. Notwithstanding this valuable salvage, the calamity was one to be for ever universally deplored; for not only did all the old charters of the Mercian kings perish in the conflagration, but hundreds of other important historical documents as well. On this sad occasion we read of relief being

Church Vestments.

sent to the monks in the shape of "money, wheat, oxen, hogs, etc;" and that "even Juliana, a poor woman of Weston, gave a large "quantity of wound thread to sew the vestments of the monks."

However trifling such a record as the latter may appear to some, we are disposed to regard it as a striking proof of the reverence in which such things were generally held in these early simple-minded times, when a laic, whose poverty was great enough to be remarked, tendered what, from her, must have been so munificent an offering, for the seemly keeping of the dress of the priestly office.

To enumerate a tithe of the vestiary splendour which comes before us relating to Croyland would leave us no room for a glance at some of the marvels of sacerdotal grandeur contained in the vestments of different progressive periods belonging to other churches.

Yet, ere we leave our much-loved Croyland Abbey, we are impelled to remark on the gift of Lawrence Chateres, the cook, of—"The black vestment wrought scripturis aureis," for officiating in at funerals, "valued at 26*l*.," which was an enormous sum in those days. And again, our attention is called to the gift of Brother Richard Woxbridge, of—

"The purple vestment sprinkled with gold flowers, two copes, "and a chasuble with tunics;" and to that of the good Abbat Upton, who, early in the fifteenth century, among other sacred and costly things, bestowed on his church—

"A red cope ornamented with gold and jewels, commonly called "'Ibi et Ubi,' valued at 100 marks; a vestment ornamented with "the arms of England and France quarterly, with copes of the "same workmanship, which also cost 100 marks; and silk em- "broidered with falcons of gold, enough to make seven copes, "which Abbat John Lytlington, his successor, made up."

Their Origin, Use, and Ornament.

Finally, it would be an injustice to this same Abbat Lytlington were we to dismiss Croyland without mention of his emulation of Richard Upton in exemplary benefactions to the monastery. He gave to it no fewer than nine copes of cloth of gold, embroidered in curious *feather*-work, and valued at 240*l*.; besides a suit of vestments of red and gold, consisting of three copes, with a chesible and three tunics, which cost 160*l*. These two sums being equivalent to 6000*l*. in money of the present day.

Every page which we have turned in research for our subject has kept us lingering over it with as much reverence for, as interest in, the people who, whatever might sometimes have been their shortcomings as men to men, through those troubled ages of persecution, invasion, bloodshed, and every species of fearful worldly warfare, from the apostolic times to far into the sixteenth century, persistently and undeviatingly observed all the solemnities due to God and our blessed Redeemer in the services of the Church; and contributed to, and maintained in becoming splendour, every appointment of the sacred office of the Holy Eucharist, as a first and last duty and privilege of the Christian profession.

Cheering, too, is it to find, that whether of the priesthood or of the world, that man who was esteemed most excellent in other relations of life, was ever the one to busy himself most about things meet and magnificent for the worship of God in His Church.

Of such, may we suppose, was Garinus, Abbat of St. Alban's, who, when all the chalices in England were called for to ransom King Richard the First from the Germans, redeemed those belonging to his monastery by the ready payment of 200 marks.[*] He also gave to the abbey that wonderful purple chasuble, so richly ornamented with figures of birds, and embroidery in fine pearls, that no just value could be set upon it.

[*] An old English coin—13*s*. 4*d*. sterling.

Church Vestments.

It was this good man too, who, dying late in the twelfth century, left 100 marks for the renewal of the front of the church. One of his successors, Thomas de la Mare, in the middle of the fourteenth century, was even more munificent in his gifts to the abbey. It is said that he spent enormously on sacred plate and vestments, and that three mitres alone cost him 100*l.*

Then we read of Godfrey de Croyland, who gave to Gaucelinus, one of the cardinals who rested at Peterborough, on his return from his mission of peace to the Scots on the part of King Edward, "a cope of gold cloth richly embroidered, and "purchased at 100 marks sterling."

By the records of Wells Cathedral, the foundation of which was almost coeval with Glastonbury Abbey, we are informed of great gifts bequeathed to it in the fifteenth century by Bishop Beckington; including four very costly vestments, 400*l.* to buy copes, a bishop's chair with cushions, and other ornaments. The adjacent abbey of Bath was also worthily remembered in his will; for, besides much valuable plate, he left to it thirty copes and other vestments.

The sacred robes contained in Old St. Paul's in the thirteenth century were as rich as they were numerous. In the inventory of the contents of the treasury in this church, made A.D. 1295, Dugdale signalizes, among other treasures—

"Nine mitres, some of them set with precious stones.

"Nine pairs of rich sandals.

"Eight croziers.

"Ten rich cushions.

"*One hundred copes*, most or all of them of the most costly "silks, many embroidered, and many of cloth of gold and tissue, "besides most curious needlework and imagery.

Their Origin, Use, and Ornament.

"Eighteen amices; and *one hundred vestments* or chasubles, "with proportionate stoles, maniples, tunicks, dalmaticks, albes, "corporals, canopies, etc."

We contemplate with natural wonder the profusion and costliness of the vestments alone, after the manner just described, belonging to our principal cathedrals and churches, when that "most dread, victorious, sovereign lord, King Henry the Eighth" issued his royal order for the surrender of their sacred effects to his impious will.

No true Christian at any period could wish to realize the cruel acts of demolition committed in Christian temples in that thirty-first year of that most dread king's reign. It is enough to know that nothing was held too sacred for his unworthy grasp. The golden chalice was profanely snatched from the hands of the priest officiating before God's holy altar, robbed of its jewels, and then melted down to be converted into coin. Costly mitres by the hundred were broken up for the sake of the pearls and precious stones that garnished them; and the hallowed robes of the Eucharistic sacrifice were rent by lawless hands, and their beautiful needlework designs defaced and mutilated, that the rare stuffs used in their formation might be turned into money, to satisfy the lust of one unjust man's avarice.

After reading the inventories taken in 1539 of the sacerdotal possessions of the monasteries in England, we find ourselves ready to search everywhere, with the hope of meeting with the merest shred by which we may recognise some one or other of the sumptuous robes enumerated in those richly-filled lists.

Such as were comprised in that gift of Cardinal Beaufort, to Winchester, of the "cope of needlework, wrought with gold and "pearls;" and the "one chysible, two tymasyles, and parel of y^e "albes of ye same work;" or but one of those countless suits of

Church Vestments.

"chesible, tunicles, copes, albes, and stoles," described so fully in the account of Peterborough.

Then again, from those copious lists of Lincoln Abbey, what might it not serve us, could we but see, even in a faded and tattered condition, but one of those " six copes of red velvet—
" one suit—broidered with angels, with the Scripture, 'Da glo-
" riam Deo,' with orphreys of needlework; of the which four
" had four Evangelists in the morses, and the fifth a Lamb in
" the morse, and the sixth a white rose and an image in the
" morse." Or the " cope of red velvet, broidered with flowers
" and angels of gold, and two of them having this Scripture,
" 'Sanctus;' in the morse, a tower; in the hood, the Salutation
" of Our Lady."

We have sat picturing to ourselves the great beauty of that gift of its sometime treasurer to Lincoln of the "white cloth " chasuble, broidered with images and angels in gold, which had " the Trinity worked in the back, with the Holy Ghost repre-" sented in pearl, and divers pearls in other images." The Eucharistic garment, the chasuble, is here clearly distinguished in richness from the dalmatics, or tunacles, as they are set down; for they are described as "of the same suit, *without pearls*." It is also worthy of note that such gifts almost invariably included, as we find it here, the whole suit of robes for the three officiating priests at the grand mass, viz.: the chasuble, two dalmatics, three albes, and three amices, with corresponding stoles and maniples.

Of the many munificent offerings of entire suits of vestments to Lincoln's wealthy wardrobe, we have singled out the following, as instancing the thought and means bestowed on the ministers of the altar by noble ladies of bygone times.

A gift of the Countess of Westmoreland is recorded as—" A

Their Origin, Use, and Ornament.

"red chesable of cloth of gold, with branches of gold, and the orphreys of green cloth, with two tunacles and three albes," etc.

And one from the Duchess of Lancaster, as—"A chesable of red bawdkin, with orphreys of gold with leopards, powdered with black trefoils, with two tunacles and three albes of the same suit, with all their apparels." While still further is the same liberal hand commemorated by—"Twenty fair copes, every one of which had wheels of silver in the hoods. And a chesable of red velvet with Catherine wheels of gold, with two tunacles and three albes, with all the apparels of the same suit."

Some very chaste examples of ancient English vestments exist in the possession of different members of our Catholic nobility and gentry; but, with few exceptions, these old sacred robes are now jealously kept from exhibition, with reverence, and a sort of atoning care for the neglect and ill-usage of three long centuries of scorn and condemnation. In the Great Exhibition of 1862 some of these were shown; one of them a cope of fourteenth-century work, belonging to Mount St. Mary's, Chesterfield, which Dr. Rock thus described:—

"No. 3,002. A very rich crimson velvet cope, of great beauty as a specimen of English needlework embroidered in gold, with subjects much after the fashion of the Syon vestment, and most admirably executed, but without any heraldry about it. One striking peculiarity is, that the angels carry stars in their hands or lying on their laps. This incident refers to the subject figured in the centre part on the back—the coming to Bethlehem of the three wise men, wearing crowns of kings, the foremost of whom is pointing with his outstretched right hand up to the leading star a little way off, above them. From some remnants it would seem that once certain parts of this

Church Vestments.

"cope were thickly studded with seed pearls, and from its profu-
"sion of gold, so unstintedly embroidered all over it, and its
"rich velvet of so deep a pile and ruby tone of colour, it must
"have been a gorgeous vestment in its day.

"As we behold it now, it furnishes us with one out of so many
"sad instances of the vandalism by which thousands of such
"admirable art-works of the English needle have been snatched
"away. The creature who once owned this precious cope cut
"it up piecemeal, and gave parts away. Some of it was ruth-
"lessly employed as the covering for a cushion, and heedlessly
"knocked about. Not long ago a man, the Rev. W. Clifford,
"of wider heart and warmer feelings for his country's mediæval
"productions, sought out with untiring labour, and got together
"as many shreds as possible of this fine old English embroidery;
"and after great toil joined them as well as might be, filling up
"the gaps with coloured sketches of the wanting fragments,
"done in excellent taste upon the new linen lining of the restored
"cope."

One other of the ancient vestments in the Exhibition at this time so impressed us by its beauty and historical associations, that we must quote it as described by the above accomplished pen. It was sent from Stonyhurst College :—

"No. 3,005. A magnificent cope of cloth of gold, figured
"with bold, widely-spreading foliage dotted with small gold
"spots, and ornamented all about with portcullises crowned and
"red roses. The lower hem is bordered with collars of SS
"and portcullises; and no doubt this is one of 'the whole suit
"of vestments and coopies of cloth of gold tissue, wrought
"with our badges of red roses and portcullises, the which we of
"late caused to be made at Florence, in Italy,' which our
"King Henry the Seventh, in his will, bequeathed 'to God and

Their Origin, Use, and Ornament.

"St. Peter, and to the abbot and prior and convent of our "monastery of Westminster,' etc.—*Testamenta Vetusta*, ed. "Nicolas, t. i., p. 33. Perhaps the design of this cope was "furnished by Torrigiano, and, through his procurement, the "whole and large set of vestments was woven at Florence. The "orphrey and hood are of poor English embroidery, and "unworthy of the cope, and in all likelihood not the originals. "Florentine tissue of the end of the fifteenth or beginning of "the sixteenth century."

The cope belonging to Sir Robert Throckmorton, also exhibited in 1862, was very fine: it was of purple velvet, powdered with double-headed eagles, beautifully embroidered in English work of the fifteenth century, with much gold about the orphrey, the hood, and the morse. Very good photographs of this cope, and of some other vestments of like beauty, are to be had at South Kensington.

We have enjoyed the privilege of restoring, or, more properly, preserving in our time many sacred garments, interesting and old as some of those just described.

Among them, a chasuble of the fourteenth century, belonging to Hengrave Hall, where it had been for ages a cherished heirloom of one of the oldest and most honourable baronetcies in Suffolk. Lord Petre also possesses a vestment of great antiquity and beauty, which some fifteen years ago received much of our care and attention; —— Silvertop, Esq., of Minster Acres, another.

We could name many others which have an equal claim upon our veneration; but without descriptions, for which we have not space, a mere enumeration of all the ancient vestments we have had the happiness to pass our working fingers over, would be lauding ourselves, and bringing no profit to our readers.

Church Vestments.

One of these fine old records in needlework must not, however, be passed over. It consisted of some vestments which were submitted to us a few years since by J. Baker Gabb, Esq., of Abergavenny. They were brought from the old religious house of Perthîr, where, in the most retired part of Monmouthshire, the English Franciscans preserved in penal times many most curious relics of better days.

They are said, with some degree of probability, to have been used originally in the very ancient parish church of St. John, at Abergavenny, now no longer a church, but the grammar-school of the town.

The most curious of these ancient embroidered robes is a chasuble of mixed work of the fourteenth and fifteenth centuries; probably effected, when the embroidery was transferred from its primitive ground, by the indiscriminate use of the needlework of two vestments of different periods, with a view to making one chasuble superlatively rich in ornament; or possibly commenced in one generation, and carried through some others to its completion, as was most common in mediæval times, when a piece of church-work was always in hand by some member, or members, of nearly every family.

If the task was left undone when its originators were called away, it was piously proceeded with by the next branch, who again might not be spared to its accomplishment. Still, a succeeding member would take it up, and so on to its consummation.

In this manner we can as well account for a mixture of styles in sacred needlework, as we can for the like in fine architectural structures, which are so rarely found to have been begun and finished in one man's generation.

On the vestment in question, the fourteenth century is illustrated by a powdering of cherubs on wheels, lily-pots, and fleur-

Their Origin, Use, and Ornament.

de-lis. The fifteenth century is evidenced by the wide Latin cross, displaying the Crucifixion, with angels receiving the blood, from the arms and side of our Lord, in chalices.

Beneath the Calvary are canopied figures, as upon the pillar in front, which is also powdered by Ely flowers, gracefully enriched by scrolls of gold. Its ground is crimson velvet, now somewhat faded, to which it has evidently been transferred a century or more ago, and the lovely work most cruelly maltreated in the process.

The original design had, doubtless, been spread over a full and majestic chasuble, but it is cut up on all sides to accommodate it to the miserably narrow shape of the eighteenth century, upon which it comes before us. The mischievous scissors have gone hissing, as though very Pagans had guided them, through every symbol dear to Christian eyes, and have even cut the lower canopied figure of the dorsal cross in half, to make the work fit *nicely* round the stunted garment of this epoch of ugliness.*

The embroidery had been tolerably well preserved, and simply required mending here and there; in other respects it remains as when we first saw it, and as shown on Plates 12 and 13.

The work upon another of these chasubles is altogether of the fifteenth century, and a fine example of its time. The ground, upon which we found it, had been a superb crimson and gold brocade velvet, the pile of which crumbled under the touch,

---

* "When the ancient cathedral church of Waterford was demolished for the purpose of "erecting the present wretched pile of building, a complete set of cloth-of-gold vestments "were discovered, of the most exquisite design and enrichments. These were given to the "Catholic bishop and clergy of the time, and being in a sufficient state of preservation for "use, they actually cut the chasubles to the modern French form, and sliced out whole "images from the needlework orphreys. One set of these vestments in their present dis- "figured state were presented by the Earl of Shrewsbury to St. Mary's College, Oscott, and "present, among the other ecclesiastical antiquities, a striking evidence of ancient excellence "and modern degeneracy."—*Pugin*, 1844.

Church Vestments.

although, the gold woven through it, rested bright and perfect on the threadbare surface. As to the needlework, whether of gold or silk, it tenaciously held together, requiring little more from us than a new foundation, to restore to it its true value for its exalted purpose.

The figures are nearly perfect, and a rebus of "R. W." and the *tun*, at the top of the pillar in front of the vestment, is remarkable as a peculiarity frequently observable in Church Embroidery of this period.*

Beneath is the figure of a bishop fully vested for the Mass, but not he whose name is given by rebus, as there is a nimbus round the head; on his finger is the episcopal ring, and in his hand he holds the pastoral staff. The two other figures on the pillar are St. John the Evangelist and St. Andrew.

Upon the cross above the Crucifix of our blessed Lord is the descending Dove; and below the Calvary, the blessed Virgin and Child, exquisitely wrought.

The arms at the bottom of the cross enable us, assisted by one well versed in heraldry, to trace somewhat of the history of this beautiful vestment.

The arms are described as:—

"Proper (divided down the centre).

"*Baron and femme.*

"Baron quartering.

" 1. Radcliffe.

" 2. Fitzwalter, gold, a fesse between two chevrons, red.

" 3. Burnell, silver, a lion rampant, argent crowned.

" 4. Derwentwater.

* In Dugdale's Inventory of Lincoln we come upon "a cope of green velvet, broidered "with lilies, with an orphrey of needlework, with a morse with a *ton*, and a branch of hay-"*thorn*, having this scripture in the morse: 'Orate pro anima Roberti *Thornton*;' and in the "hood: 'Pater de cœlis,' etc., with the Trinity."

Their Origin, Use, and Ornament.

"Femme quartering.
" 1. First quarter, quartering France and England.
" 2. Bohun, Earl of Hereford.
" 3. Bohun, Earl of Northampton.
" 4. Stafford."

Then we are told that "Henry Stafford, Earl of Buckingham, "beheaded by Richard the Third, left (with other children) a "daughter Elizabeth, married to Robert, Lord Fitzwalter, who "was a Radcliffe." And by this their shield, Radcliffe impaling Stafford, the work of the chasuble is fixed at the time of Henry the Seventh, at latest.

For the illustration and particulars of the two vestments we have just detailed, with that of one other of fifteenth-century work equally fine, which we transferred to a rich green lama, we are deeply indebted to J. Baker Gabb, Esq., who for our book's sake has had them photographed under his own direction. They are all now under the care of, and used by, the Benedictine Fathers at Abergavenny, who have succeeded the English Franciscans in the mission, that order having become extinct.

Beautiful specimens of ancient sacerdotal embroidery are now shown in the South Kensington Museum.

The best and most numerous of these are from Germany, brought hither by Dr. F. Bock, who, laudably inspired by our enthusiasm in collecting early examples of Church needlework, has energetically searched every available corner in his own country to place before us works of Catholic art worthy of any Christian land.

There are also a few Italian relics in the collection of the Museum; but, and we blush to write a truth which speaks volumes for our vandalism, scarcely any that are notable are English. It is hard to have to own to our poverty in this respect, when we remember how zealously and industriously our pious ancestors toiled for the honour and enrichment of the Church and its posterity, and how wealthy our monasteries were, at the close of the fifteenth century, in works of value, such as all nations coveted to possess.

Apart from every other consideration but the love of art in sacred needlework, we could wish that William the Conqueror had been the immediate predecessor of Henry the Eighth. For, we know how William enriched his Normandy churches by vestments taken from us,* and had he come with the same predatory tastes at the period we name, we might now be blessing his memory for unwittingly removing from harm's way, for the benefit of future generations, countless exquisite English productions of the needle, of the thirteenth and fourteenth centuries: that epoch which is literally dazzling in manuscript and history, with the beauty in the design and execution of its ecclesiastical ornament.

Every possible variety of manipulation in the "cunning work" of the needle practised by the pious of the past may be seen and studied, with profit and edification, in the collection of treasures alluded to at South Kensington.

The shapes of the different garments upon which these embroideries are disposed must, in most instances, be disregarded, as very few of them will be found in accordance with their primitive type, and still fewer of the needlework subjects can be recognised on the fabrics upon which they were first placed. Some of the present foundations are not coeval with their

---

* "Well could this royal robber William afford to make presents of rich vestments to the "churches of Normandy, when he stole them so unscrupulously from Anglo-Saxon monas- "teries: from Waltham Abbey alone he carried away ten most splendid chasubles, as we "find in 'Vitâ et Miracle. Haroldi,' Harleian MS. 3766."—*Vide* Dr. Rock, "*Church of our* "*Fathers.*"

Their Origin, Use, and Ornament.

elaborate ornamentation, and much of the embroidery will be found mutilated, after the manner of the Abergavenny work, and frequently the original design broken up, if not perverted, in the construction of a cope from an altar-covering, a chasuble from a reredos hanging, or stoles and maniples from the apparels of dalmatics.

This has nothing to do with the lovely *stitchery*, which, as we have just said, comprehends every wonder in the curious art, which the most ambitious Church needlewoman need desire to compass.

That orphrey from a chasuble, executed for one of the Dukes of Cleves—1460—is surpassingly fine. With only this, and the Sion cope, within reach for imitation, as great things in sacerdotal embroidery might be achieved as ever yet were done.

We sent forth our recently published work as a pioneer, to prepare the way with practical instructions for the execution of every kind of ecclesiastical needlework upon which, at any future time, we might be impelled to write.

To repeat those instructions here would be simply to fill two books with the same matter; an absurdity which all will recognise, without further comment from us.

We intend devoting a little chapter to each article employed in the priestly office; tracing it from its origin, describing the changes and modifications which have been made in its form, and, finally, giving simplified instructions for the adornment of each object in appropriate design and needlework, for the detailed accomplishment of which we refer our readers to "Church Em-" broidery, Practically Illustrated."

As in that book, we here write only of what appertains to the Church in England. Catholic worship is undoubtedly the same all over the world; but in the forms and style of ornament of the

Church Vestments.

priestly robes there are slight differences, characteristic of the people in every land, about which we need have no concern. Insomuch as we may rest satisfied that the knowledge of the true faith, with every sacred appointment necessary for its solemn observance, came to us as soon as it did to any other nation, and if we endeavour to follow closely, according to our lights, the dresses and ceremonies deemed indispensable for a Christian ritual in England, when the penalty of its performance was martyrdom, which saintly men and women gloried to earn, we may not seek to know, even in this nineteenth century, what is being done for God's holy service elsewhere.

We began this introductory chapter with the words of the Highest of all high authorities for our theme, and, as a fitting conclusion to it, give the following gracefully written extract from "Annals of the Virgin Saints":—

"It has ever been the end and aim of Holy Church to
" symbolize the heavenly by the earthly; to use the beauty and
" majesty of this world in leading on her children to the yet un-
" seen glory of the 'many mansions' prepared for them in the
" next. She has pressed into her service the precious things of
" sea and land; she has hallowed that which had otherwise been
" abused to worldly pomp; she has dared 'to inherit the earth.'

"She leaves not the snowdrop in its spotless loveliness to return
" with a smile from its laurel hedge-shelter the faint caresses of a
" February sun: it must deck the high altars when we comme-
" morate *her* purification, who was herself pure beyond all the
" daughters of Eve.*

"So with gold and silver, and the gems of the mine, they
" blaze in the chalice and the paten, they are curiously wrought

---

* "The lily may not hide itself in the modest garden-bed, for it is the flower of virgins, the "symbol of the pure in heart."

Their Origin, Use, and Ornament.

" in the mitre and the clasped cope, they glitter in the pastoral
" staff and processional cross; so with the work of the needle,
" the hanging, the frontal, the corporal, and the veil, all exercise
" the patient skill of the artist, all occupy the quiet hours of the
" convent.
     * * * "Thus, then, the spoils of nature came to her
" (the Church), thus her children offer in her service the best,
" the brightest of God's gifts. Why? but in some faint degree
" to set forth that land which eye hath not seen nor ear heard,
" to allure the wanderer from the riches of the earth, by means
" of those very riches to impress on the enemy's gold the stamp
" of the 'King of Kings.' "

II.

THE AMICE.

THE Amice was not brought into use until the eighth century, from which period till now it has been the first vestment put on by the minister over his cassock, when robing for the Mass.

In the tenth century it was sometimes called the "super-humerale," which would imply that it belonged more to the shoulders than to the neck, and from its non-appearance upon illuminated figures of that time, it is justly supposed that it was, at first, drawn away from the neck to be spread about the shoulders, under the alb. Scarcely any paintings or effigies of robed ecclesiastics, done in the middle ages, present the amice as covering the neck. In nearly every instance the apparel of the amice is turned down to meet the top of the chasuble, and the throat of the wearer left exposed. This is evidenced by most of the ancient figures shown on Plates 6, 9, and 30.

When a sub-deacon is ordained, according to the Roman rite, the bishop invests him with the amice by drawing it up over his head; and, anciently, the amice was worn as a hood from the sacristy to the altar; upon reaching which, the priest threw the garment back upon his shoulders, till the end of the Mass, when he again shrouded his head on retiring. This is still the custom with the Dominicans and Capuchins, and is also observed

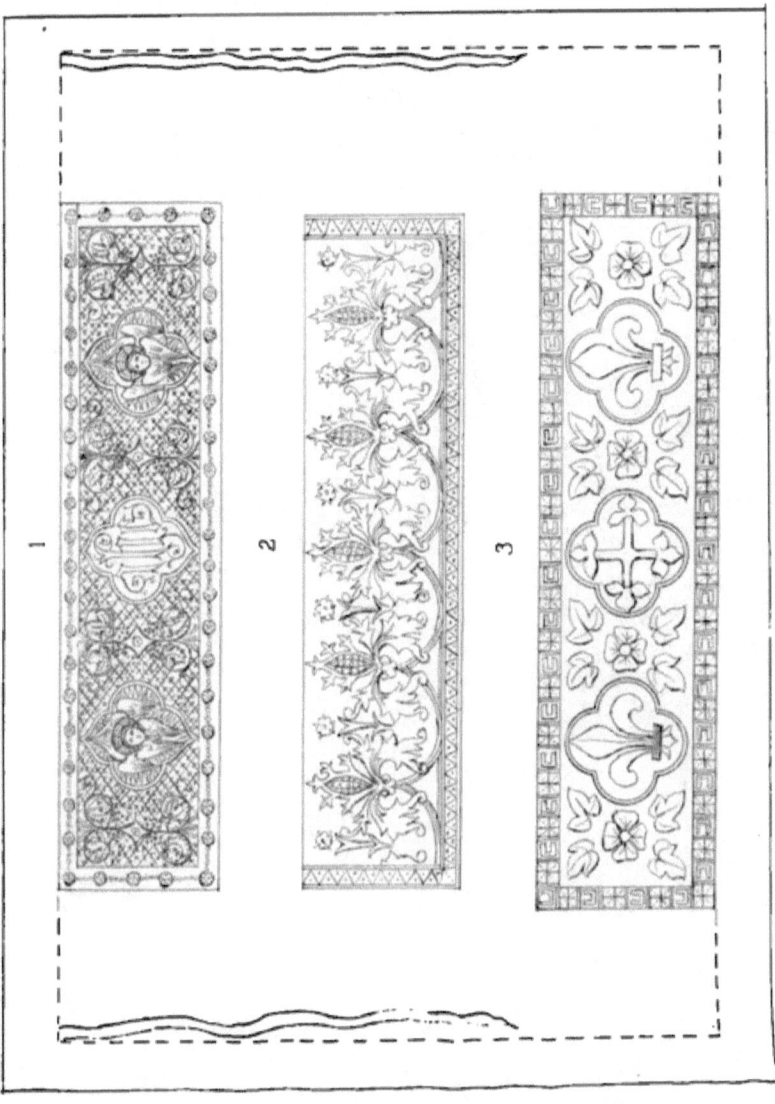

Nº 1 AN AMICE WITH ITS APPAREL.
Nºs 2 & 3. DESIGNS FOR APPARELS FOR OTHER AMICES.

The Amice.

in some places abroad. We are told too, that, formerly, the amice was used as a hood by the clergy who walked in processions, as shrine-bearers or otherwise, when they went beyond the precincts of the church, or through the fields, or the streets of the city.

According to the old Sarum ritual, churchmen of the minor class might wear the amice; even "the boys who bore the "tapers, the thurifers, and the acolyte who carried the Cross, "were all clad in alb and *amice*."

That the amice was originally intended to cover the head there can be no doubt. By writers of the thirteenth century the term *amice* is made synonymous with words that could only apply to a covering for the head; and, even so late as the memorable year 1539, when Holy Church was bidden to cast all her sacred treasures into the rapacious king's coffers, the amice was set down as "kerchief,"—derived from the French "couvre "chief," a head-covering.

Hence it was, and still is, assumed by Catholic ministers as symbolical of the helmet of salvation, suggested by the exhortation of St. Paul, Ephes. vi. 11, 17.

The priest, when preparing for the Eucharistic Service, rests the amice for an instant upon the top of his head, while he recites the following beautiful prayer:—

"Place upon my head, O Lord, the helmet of salvation, that "I may be enabled to repel all the fiery darts of the wicked "one."

He then arranges the garment over his shoulders, and crossing its strings over his breast, and securing them around his body, assumes the alb.

The *apparel* of the amice has now to be noticed. In Anglo-Saxon times these *apparels* are described as gorgeous in the extreme, not only with rich embroidery on costly grounds, but with gems and enamels set about the elaborate work of the needle. Not unfrequently, we are told, was the amice of a prelate apparelled with thin plates of beaten gold, " studded with " pearls, and sparkling with precious stones."

The ancient apparel was a border attached to one of the lateral edges of the amice, the plain part of which, when turned down, left the apparel to form a magnificent collar above the chasuble. As see Plate 11, on the figure of Thomas de la Mare, abbot of St. Albans.

The apparel of the amice is rapidly coming into use again; and, as formerly, may have any amount of work and rich material expended upon it, providing that it be made after its prototype, *i. e.*, in strict harmony as to colour and quality with the vestments of the day.

In these later times we have frequently seen, in the absence of needlework, a rich woven lace, like that employed for the apparels of albs, sewn along the upper edge of the amice: there is no objection to this substitute for embroidery, although the latter is undoubtedly preferable.

The amice should be made of pure fine linen, and should be shaped as an oblong square, measuring 36 inches by 25. It should have a small cross worked in the centre upon its upper edge, and strings sewn at each end, long enough to cross over the breast and encircle the body.

Whether the apparel of the amice be of needlework or of lace, it must be applied to the linen in such a way, that it may be readily detached when the garment requires washing.

The *coif*, or *coyfe*, anciently placed upon the sovereign's head at his coronation, for the conservation of the unction, has sometimes been called an amice. This is a great error; for

The Amice.

such a cloth is totally distinct from that worn by the priesthood.

The following, extracted from the "Church of our Fathers," is from the account of the coronation of Edward the Sixth, and clearly indicates the true purpose of the *coif*, as it also shows the use of linen gloves for the retention of the unction upon the hands :—

"After the king's enonction, the archbishop dried every place "of the same with cotton and lynnen cloth . . . puting on the "king's hands a paire of lynnen gloves, and on his head a lynnen "coyfe." On Plate 1, is given an amice with apparel.

Since writing the above, Dr. Rock has privileged us to insert the following account of an ancient amice preserved at South Kensington, from his yet unpublished "Descriptive Catalogue" of "Textile Fabrics;" comprised in the "Collection of Church "Vestments, dresses, silk stuffs, needlework, and tapestries forming "that section of the Museum":—

"8307

"Linen Amice, with its apparel of crimson silk, to which are "sewed small ornaments in silver and silver-gilt. German, "fifteenth century, 4 feet 2 inches by 1 foot 11 inches.

"The example of linen in this amice will, for the student of "mediæval antiquities and manufactures, be of great service, "showing, as it does, what we are to understand was the kind of "stuff meant by canvas in old accounts which speak of that "material so often as bought for making albs, surplices, and "other linen garments used in the ceremonial of the Church. "The crimson ornament of silk, sprinkled with large spangle-like "plates of silver-gilt, and struck with a variety of patterns, is "another of various instances to show how the goldsmith's craft

Church Vestments.

" in the middle ages was brought into play for ornaments upon
" silk and other textiles; and the liturgical student will be glad
" to see in this specimen an instance, now so very rare, of an old
" amice, with its strings, but more especially its apparel, in its
" place; about which see ' Church of our Fathers,' t. i. 463."

The Alb.

III.

THE ALB.

"And one of the elders answered, saying unto me, What are these which are arrayed in white robes? and whence came they?

"And I said unto him, Sir, thou knowest. And he said unto me, These are they which came out of great tribulation, and have washed their robes, and made them white in the blood of the Lamb."

REVELATION, *ch.* vii., *ver.* 13, 14.

THE Alb is the next garment, after the amice, put on over the cassock, alike by Pope, prelate, priest, deacon, and sub-deacon, when robing for the Mass.

That coloured albs of cloth of gold, velvet, and silk, most richly worked, were formerly used, we know perfectly well; for in nearly every inventory of Church treasures made A.D. 1539, albs of this description are profusely laid down, and in some cases minutely described.

In the Peterborough list of vestments we count considerably more than three hundred albes of *divers* colours, materials, and ornamentation. Some are noted as—

"*Embroidered with vines.*" Others,

"With *Peter-keys.*" Several,

"With *crowns* and *moons.*" Many more,

"With *apples of cloth of gold.*" There are—

"Six called the *kydds.*"

"Six the *meltons.*"

"Six the *doggs.*"

Church Vestments.

"One the *burgon*." While of red albes for Passion Week alone, twenty-seven are enumerated.

We also find albs included as a part of every set of vestments named in these inventories, and corresponding in their materials and decoration with the other garments. As, for instance, in this same Peterborough inventory, we meet with the following suits, to which the albs just named evidently belonged:—

"One suit of *Peter-keys*, with two copes."
"One suit of the *doggs*, with two copes."
"One suit of the *meltons*, so called, with eight copes."
"One suit called the *kydds*, with four copes."
"One suit called the *vines*."
"Two copes called the *burgons*," etc.

Other records satisfy us that the custom of making the albs assimilate in richness with the robes with which they were worn prevailed long before the close of Henry the Seventh's reign.

Lord Wm. Smith, bishop of Lincoln, A.D. 1495, gave to the abbey "A chesable, cloth of tishew, with two tunacles, and three "copes of the same suit, with costly orphreys of gold, and "images of needlework; and *three albes*, with the *apparel of the* "*same.*"

It might justly be considered tedious, as unnecessary, to cite further proofs of the practice of wearing the richly-adorned coloured alb in early mediæval times; and although, as we have endeavoured to show, the garment made after this fashion was extensively brought into use before the Protestant era, yet we doubt not for a single moment that it was originally pure white, as its name, from the Latin *alba*, implies, and probably adopted by the first worshippers in the Christian Church, in imitation of the white raiment of the blessed in heaven, so continually alluded to by the Evangelist St. John. Indeed, we are led to believe

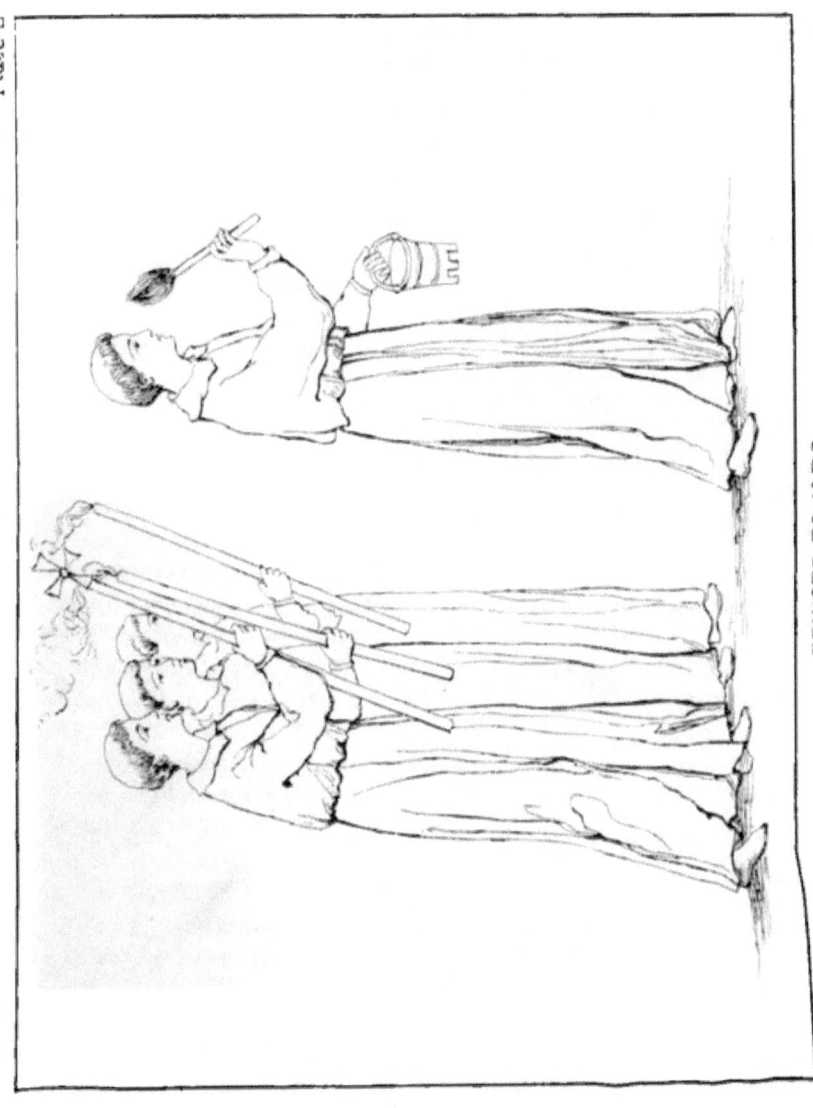

PRIESTS IN ALBS
From Procession of St Alban's Shrine

The Alb.

that the white linen alb was never relinquished for the costly coloured robe of that name, but worn beneath the latter. We have no written authority for this conclusion; but in old manuscripts discover figures clothed in apparelled albs, and above them coloured garments, which are certainly neither tunicles nor dalmatics. For not only do they take the form of the white alb, but we know that, from the subject of the picture, the figures could only be vested in albs.

The alb, "the closely-fitting fine white lawn garment, reaching "from the neck to the feet, and confined by a girdle," is faithfully pictured on Plate 2, in the procession of St. Alban's shrine, copied from the original of Matthew Paris in the Cottonian library. These figures show the alb in its most simple and beautiful form, and as we would like to see it worn by every priest at the present day. Even the very earliest kind of ornamentation of the alb, the border around the bottom, is absent from these; and yet how graceful and dignified they are, and how literally they resemble what we can imagine was suggested to the first Christians, as the raiment worn by the seven angels of the Apocalypse, who " came out of the temple clothed in pure " and white linen, and having their breasts girded with golden " girdles."

Anciently it was the custom of the Christian Church to solemnize the holy rite of Baptism on the eve of Easter-day, when to each of the newly baptized was given a pure white robe, to be worn through the eight following days. The Easter week was called *Alba*, and the Octave of Easter-day, when the baptized put off their white dresses, was called "Dominica in albis de-" positis."

The first coloured decoration of the alb was carried all round the lower part of the robe, and consisted of bands or stripes of scarlet, which were often made of silk with fringes of gold. Anastasius the librarian enumerates several albs of this enriched character which, among other gifts, were offered by the King of the Saxons to the church of St. Peter at Rome. Figs. 1 and 4, on Plate 9, show the most primitive form of the border round the alb; while fig. 3, on the same Plate, and fig. 1, on Plate 8, illustrate the next stage in the adornment of the originally plain white garment.* The square-sided pieces of rich stuffs called *apparels* placed before and behind at the lower part of the alb, and upon the sleeves, were not brought into use until that period in the thirteenth century when ornament of all kinds began to be so lavishly bestowed upon every exalted object, whether sacred or profane.

These apparels of the priest's alb were either formed of the same gorgeous material as the chasuble; or they were beautifully embroidered in geometrical figures and scrolls on costly gold fabrics; or they were figured in rare needlework with holy subjects, graphically descriptive of the high festival upon which the particular alb was to be expressly worn.

Latterly, the practice has become general of forming the apparels of the alb of rich silk lace, woven for the purpose. There being no arbitrary rule for the dimensions of these woven apparels, they are made of various sizes and widths, but always of an oblong shape.

Fourteen inches by 8 are good medium proportions for the skirt apparels, and 6 inches by 4 for those of the wrist. Occasionally we have seen an apparel on the breast of the robe,

---

* When Adelina de Bellmont went with the wife of the Conqueror to visit the abbey of St. Evroul, she presented to the church "an alb richly adorned with orfrais." The chronicler, Vitalis, further says, that this garment was especially worn by the priest at the celebration of the Mass.

The Alb.

an addition by some believed to be essential to complete the figure of the five wounds of our Lord, asserted as originally symbolized by the apparels on the alb.

This tradition may, or may not, be accepted. It is rendered doubtful to us by the fact that an apparel was at one time sewn on the upper part of the *back* of the garment, as well as upon the breast; thus showing *six* separate pieces, and greatly confusing the beautiful idea of the figure of the *five* sacred wounds.

In most churches at this moment, the alb apparels are not in general use, but are reserved for the enrichment of the garment on great festivals. As was very much the custom in ancient times.

Whether the alb has apparels or not, it is now nearly always worn by every priest, who ignores the transparent lace border, ornamented by a border of chain-stitch or other cotton embroidery, worked all round the bottom of the skirt, and about the wrists.

These borders are wrought either in red cotton or in red and blue mixed through the pattern, and sometimes, but rarely, in white cotton only.

The origin of coloured chain-stitch on the alb may perhaps be traced to the custom of embroidering the under linen garments of the people of rank in the middle ages with delicate borders of colour. The cambric shirt of the youthful Prince Arthur, eldest son of Henry the Seventh, is one among the many unique relics of antiquity belonging to Sir Edward Gage of Hengrave. This truly historical treasure, is in a most perfect condition, and exquisitely worked in a marvellously cunning stitch, and elegant pattern, with fine dark-blue silk down each seam, and about the neck and shoulders. The little collar, about 2 inches wide, is a gem in design and needlecraft.

Church Vestments.

The alb bordered, or more properly flounced, with transparent lace is a libel on the pure white robe of the primitive Christians. Even though the costliest lace be used for its adornment, yet is it deficient in the sacred simplicity of character of the original garment. But when we see those deep borders of flimsy meretricious manufacture, which many of us would disdain for window curtains, hanging about the feet of the ministers at God's altar, we fain would ask for means large enough, and hands numerous enough, to offer an alb made after the only true model to every priest who might be willing to accept it.

The magnificent alb of Point d'Alençon, presented to Pope Pius the Ninth by Eugénie, Empress of the French, is said to be the wonder of the age in lace. Not only is the pattern exquisitely beautiful, but it is the finest specimen of Point D'Alençon ever made in one piece. Its cost, as may be supposed, was enormous.

The pious spirit that prompted such a gift cannot be overestimated, for we all know that Eugénie is good as she is great; but with all reverence for the recipient, and admiration for the donor, we cannot forbear thinking that a fine lawn alb, worked by her own kind hands, would have found as much favour in the eyes of his Holiness as the costly robe of Point D'Alençon, which the mere wealth of any other empress might buy.

A curious alb in the South Kensington Museum is minutely described, as follows, by Dr. Rock, in his Catalogue of "Textile "Fabrics," already mentioned, page 29, as in course of publication:—

"8710

"Alb of white linen appareled at the cuffs, and before and "behind at the feet, with crimson and gold stuff figured with "animals and floriations of the looms of Palermo. Sicilian,

The Alb.

"fourteenth century. 5 feet 7 inches long, 4 feet across the
"shoulders, without the sleeves.

"For those curious in liturgical appliances, this fine alb of the
"mediæval period will be a valuable object of study, though
"perhaps not for imitation in the way in which it is widened at
"the waist. Its large opening at the neck—1 foot 4½ inches—
"is somewhat scalloped, but without any slit down the front, or
"gatherings, or band. On each shoulder, running down 1 foot
"3¾ inches, is a narrow piece of crochet-work inscribed in red
"letters with the names 'Jesus,' 'Maria.' The full sleeves, from
"1 foot 6 inches wide, are gradually narrowed to 6¼ inches at
"the end of the apparels at the cuffs, which are 4 inches deep,
"and edged with green linen tape. At the waist, where it is
"3 feet 10 inches, it is made, by means of gatherings upon a
"gusset embroidered with a cross-crosslet in red thread, to widen
"itself into 6 feet, or 12 feet all round. Down the middle,
"before and behind, as far as the apparels, is let in a narrow
"piece of crochet-work like that upon the shoulders, but unin-
"scribed. The two apparels at the feet—one before, the other
"behind—vary in their dimensions; one measuring 1 foot 1 inch
"by 1 foot 1¾ inches; the other, which is made up of fragments,
"1 foot by 11¾ inches. Very elaborate and freely designed is
"the heraldic pattern on the rich stuff which forms the apparels.
"The ground is of silk, now faded, but once a bright crimson,
"or a field *gules*; the figures, all in gold or *or*, are an eagle in
"demi-vol, langued, with a ducal crown, not upon, but over its
"head; above this is a mass of clouds with pencils of sun-rays
"darting from beneath them all around; higher up again, a
"collared hart lodged, with its park set between two large bell-
"shaped, seeded, drooping flowers, beneath each of which is a dog
"collared and courant. For English antiquaries, it may be

Church Vestments.

"interesting to know, that upon the mantle and kirtle in the monumental effigy of King Richard the Second, in Westminster Abbey, the hart as well as the cloud with rays are both figured as the pattern on those royal garments, and well shown in the valuable, but unfinished, 'Monumental Effigies of Great Britain,' by the late brothers Hollis.

"This alb is figured, but not well with regard to the apparels, by Dr. Bock, in his 'Geschichte der Liturgischen Gewänder des Mittelalters,' 4 Lieferung, pl. iii. fig. 1."

We have been at some pains to secure for our book the model of an alb which comes as nearly as possible to the old form we love so well. On Plate 3 it is shown. The officiating priests at the altar in the frontispiece exhibit it to advantage beneath the sacrificial robes. Subjoined are the dimensions of the correct plain lawn alb for a figure of middle height and ordinary proportions:—

10 ft. wide, and made, without gores or slope of any kind from top to bottom, of four breadths of fine lawn of 30 in. wide.

Length *behind* when made	4 ft. 9 in.
Length before	4 ft. 5 in.
Depth of shoulder band	$8\frac{1}{2}$ in.
Width of same	$1\frac{1}{4}$ in.
Length of sleeve, outside of arm . . .	2 ft. $1\frac{1}{2}$ in.
Width of sleeve at wrist, folded in two, *when made*	$6\frac{1}{2}$ in.
Width of sleeve half way up . . .	$9\frac{1}{2}$ in.
Width of sleeve at top	11 in.

Sleeve gussett $5\frac{1}{2}$ in. square, *when made*.

Length of neck-band	2 ft. $2\frac{1}{2}$ in.
Width of same	$1\frac{1}{4}$ in.

Plate 3.

THE CORRECT ALB.

The Alb.

Opening down front, which is a simple slit with a narrow hem down one side, and one rather wider to lap over on the other . . $13\frac{1}{2}$ in.
Hem of skirt and of wrist . . . . $1\frac{1}{4}$ in. wide.
Needlework border, above hem of skirt . . $\begin{cases} 2\frac{3}{4} \text{ to } 6\frac{1}{4} \text{ in.} \\ \text{wide.} \end{cases}$
„ „ above hem of sleeve . $1\frac{1}{2}$ to 3 in.
Plate 35 suggests designs for borders in chain-stitch for albs.

Church Vestments.

IV.

THE GIRDLE.

THE Girdle is used by every priest to confine his alb. In ancient times it was not only as "the curious girdle of "the ephod" made of "gold, and blue, and purple, and scarlet, "and fine twined linen," but was often richly embroidered, and embellished with precious stones.

Originally, the girdle was not formed as now of a twisted cord, but resembled in make and ornamentation the flat and somewhat broad belts or zones with which we are so familiar in illustrations of regally-arrayed figures of the middle ages, only that the latter hung down in two long ends in front of the wearer, while that of the priest terminated in front by the hook or the clasp which fastened it about the waist. The will of the Conqueror's wife contains the following bequest:—

"I give to the abbey of the Holy Trinity my tunic worked at "Winchester by Alderet's wife, and the mantle embroidered "with gold, which is in my chamber, to make a cope. Of my "two golden *girdles*, I give that which is ornamented with "emblems for the purpose of suspending the lamp before the "great altar."

In various parts of holy writ the use of the girdle is indicated and enjoined. The Eternal Father deigned to signalize, over and over again, the girdle which was to be made for Aaron, "to

The Girdle.

"minister unto Him in the priest's office." The prophet Isaiah, in his foreshadowing of the Messiah, speaks of that *righteousness* and *faithfulness*, which shall be the *girdle* of His loins.

Our blessed Lord himself exhorts His disciples to "let their "loins be girded about, and their lights burning;" and St. Paul, in his Epistle to the Ephesians, bids them stand in "the whole "armour of God, having their loins girt about with truth."

It is this girdle, with all its glorious precedents and attributes, which the holy Church, in her desire to perpetuate the use of all things that have a sacred import, orders to be worn at this day, the same as in the beginning, as a part of the sacerdotal garments in which every priest of the altar must be vested before he can officiate at the solemn service of the Mass.

Dr. Rock, in speaking of the girdle, says:—"Very appropri-
"ately is it made a portion of the ceremonial attire belonging to
"the sanctuary, and is eloquently emblematical of that chastity
"and unsullied purity with which both priest and people should
"anxiously endeavour to array themselves before they dare to
"pass the threshold of a temple sacred to the Lord of spotless
"holiness; 'Gird,' says the minister, as he binds it on, 'gird my
"reins, O Lord, with the girdle of purity; extinguish in my
"heart the fire of concupiscence; and may the flames of thy
"holy love consume every earthly affection, everything therein
"that is unworthy of thee.'"

Although a girdle of silk, of the colour of the day, is admissible, and in some places such is always used by the bishop, yet that which is in general use is white. It should never be made of anything inferior to linen thread, and should measure from $1\frac{3}{4}$ to 2 inches in circumference.

Its tassels may be 6 inches deep, inclusive of the top; its cord, 4 yards long.

Church Vestments.

The best girdles are those, at present made in some convents,* of plaited or twined linen tape, with tassels formed of the purest linen thread. The tops of these tassels should be made soft, of the solid flaxen material: upon no account must they be worked over a wooden mould.

* At the Franciscan convent at Taunton these girdles are made to perfection, as also are rochets, albs, surplices, amices, etc.

V.

THE CHASUBLE.

THE following are the different terms by which the sacrificial robe has been called since its origin.

Pænula, from the covering or cloak of that name in use among the Romans when Christianity was in its infancy. *Planeta*, from the Greek, signifying vastness in a circular form. *Chasuble*, from the Latin *casula*, meaning a little hut; and applied to the garment, from the figure being entirely enveloped by it, as in a house or dwelling.

The word *Chesible*, or Chysible, as we find it indiscriminately written in the middle ages, is of course synonymous with *Chasuble*, the now generally accepted term for the sacred vestment.

Nothing positive is known concerning the garment worn by the apostles and their priestly successors, in the performance of the Eucharistic service, during the first days of the Christian dispensation. For although the cloak of St. Paul, which he left at Troas with Carpus, is surmised by some writers to have been the holy vestment, yet there is no direct authority for regarding this as anything more than a mere probability.

The pænula was a garment of a simple circular shape, with a piece cut out of the centre to allow the head to pass through, and was made large enough to fall about in soft rich folds, while it nearly enveloped the person of the wearer. Its use in Rome succeeded that of the toga, and from its amplitude and encompassing form, it was doubtless one of the most chaste, and unassuming in appearance, of the secular robes of the period. Hence, we may understand why the early Christians adopted it as best fitted to be worn during their sacred offices; regarding it, at one and the same time, as symbolical in its roundness and fulness of the never-ending joys of the faithful followers of the Saviour, and the plenitude of the love of the Eternal Father.

Dr. Rock, in his "Church of our Fathers," beautifully expresses the symbolism of the primitive chasuble, when he writes of it as "a speaking emblem of unity in faith, being un-
" divided at the sides, and of charity, that far-reaching love for
" God and man shown by a holy life; the uppermost vestment
" of bishop and of priest, so large, so wide, and spreading itself
" all about the wearer, aptly did it betoken that virtue which,
" above all others, should ever shine out through all the actions
" of the good and worthy churchman."

It will at once be seen on Plate 4 how completely the figure within the circular chasuble was confined, and hidden as it were, until the arms were raised in sacred action, when the robe, turned up in massive folds over the shoulders, as shown on the same Plate, and the rest of the dress arranged itself naturally about the person of the priest, in a stately and majestic manner, such as few modern vestments can bring to our minds.

When the chasuble was worn thus large, the deacon held up its side, during the elevation, and other solemn parts of the service, to relieve the arms of the celebrant; and thus, an act, which was at one time really one of necessity, is now, owing to the curtailed dimensions of the vestment, practised as a mere symbol of an old usage. In former times, too, the celebrant

Plate 4.

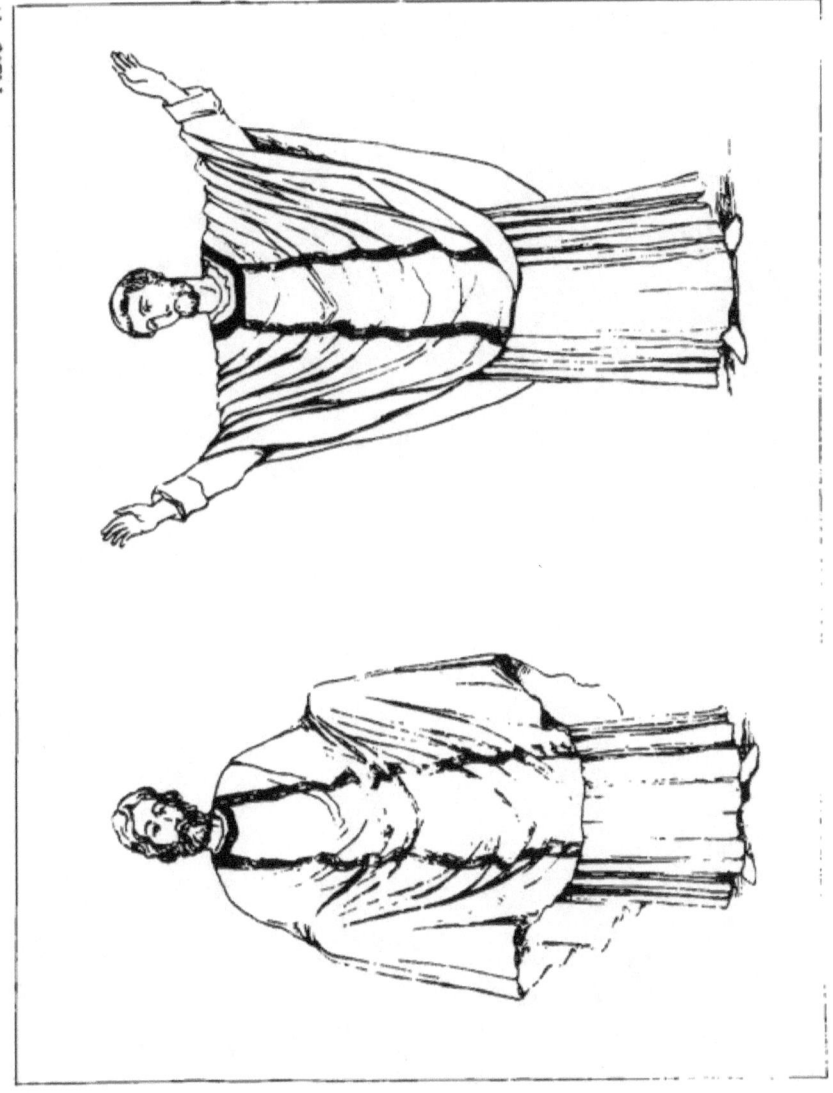

CHASUBLE OF THE EARLY CHRISTIANS

The Chasuble.

allowed the chasuble to cover him entirely, keeping his hands beneath its enveloping folds during the Confiteor; after which the assistant priests raised the sides of the vestment, and affixed the maniple to the left arm.

Some of the ancient chasubles must have been of great size, judging from such accounts as that of the Diptych Chasuble of the church of St. Apollinaris, in the city of Ravenna, which commemorated in needlework thirty-five bishops of the church of Verona, with the archangels Michael and Gabriel, besides other saints. The length of this vestment behind was 6 feet 8 inches, while the front measured 6 feet.*

In the early days of the Church, another kind of chasuble was in simultaneous use with the ordinary Eucharistic robe of that name, and from which it differed but in one particular, viz., that it was *hooded*, and appointed to be worn only during solemn processions in the open air.

We can trace this custom of wearing the hooded chasuble in England no farther than the seventh century. Probably, its use may have continued later, although we have no records left to prove the fact; for it was certainly not relinquished in France till the close of the ninth century.

The late A. W. Pugin, in his "Glossary of Architecture," published in 1844, gave us a standard for the shape and size of the principal Eucharistic vestments, which ever since has been more or less adhered to in the exercise of true taste in sacerdotal ornament.

---

* "Respecting the ancient vestment at Ravenna, of which only a few fragments now remain, its texture of silver and silk is of a later introduction into the manufacture of Church vestments than that of gold. Salmasius says that silver tissue was not made, or used in churches, till the times of the last Byzantine emperors. The chrysoclave of this vestment is, however, of gold embroidery; and the work such as must have resembled solid gold, which appears to be the general character of the old chrysoclave."—*I. W. Pugin*, 1844.

Church Vestments.

This standard was suggested by Dr. Daniel Rock: the chasuble delineated *should have been* an exact copy of one of the fourteenth century, which the Doctor met with in the Treasury of the Cathedral of Aix-la-Chapelle.*

He relates how, upon his return to England, he had a purple silk chasuble made after this fine old model, and ornamented in like manner by an orphrey of pearls; and also had the apparels for alb and amice wrought with white silk on a purple ground to match the chasuble, copying the design for these apparels from the grave brass in Westminster Abbey, of Waldeby, Archbishop of York.

These vestments were lent to Mr. Pugin, who had counterparts of them made, which were again imitated and brought into use throughout the Midland district; and until now, we were assured that it was from these the dimensions of chasuble, etc., represented as examples of the true old form, on Plate 2 of his beautiful Glossary, were actually taken.

Even the original of the chasuble above mentioned is of a date long subsequent to that when the perfectly circular vestment was worn; but it is certainly of a form equally fine, and near enough to the ancient outline to be as distinguished for its sacred purpose.

From the earliest days of the Christian priesthood till now, the chasuble has been the especial robe given to the servants of the Lord at their ordination. And no true Catholic priest, we are authorized to say, has ever yet dared to celebrate the Holy Mass

---

* We have but recently examined this vestment, and are therefore in a position to say, confidently, that it differs materially from the chasuble of the Pugin standard. The former, measuring from the neck, being 33 inches deep at the shoulder; the latter, barely 20 inches. Although the proportions laid down by Pugin constitute a fine symmetrical shape, yet we prefer its prototype, as shown, Plate 14, for its amplitude, which invests the garment with so much more dignity.

The Chasuble.

divested of this garment, consecrated for his highest office in the Church. So far back as the year 606, we are informed from the Life of St. Austin, written by Gosselinus, that " St. Augustine, the " apostle of England, at the ordination of his beloved scholar " (S. Livinus), presented him with a tender pledge and memorial " of his affection, viz., a purple chasuble, a presage of his " glorious martyrdom, bordered with gold and jewels, emblems " of Saints' virtues."—*Pugin.*

It is probable that the slight alterations effected in the chasuble from its first adoption by the priesthood to the fifteenth century were mainly owing to the progressive changes which took place in architectural detail.

If we accept this hypothesis, we have but to refer, first to manuscripts, and then to the effigies on still existing old monuments in our different cathedrals and churches, to be enabled to trace the melting away, as it were, of the round arch of the planeta of the early Roman Christians, to the elegant lines which are presented to us in the favoured vesica piscis shape of the old Eucharistic vestment of Aix-la-Chapelle.

The late A. W. Pugin, while speaking of the vesica form of the chasuble of the middle ages, suggests that, "this shape may " have been partially selected in reference to its symbolical signi- " fication of our Lord's mystical name." This conjecture is quite as reasonable as, and perhaps more consistent than, our own supposition; still, we may not be far wrong in concluding, that to reverence for a pious tradition, combined with that true taste for the beautiful, in ecclesiastical design, which certainly had attained its climax in the fourteenth century, may be ascribed the elegant and symmetrical outline of the purely Gothic chasuble.

In the "Church of our Fathers," Dr. Rock gives engravings

Church Vestments.

of two bishops of Ravenna, from mosaics of the sixth century, considering these "the earliest work of art in which the sacrificial " chasuble is unmistakably shown." These figures are exhibited on Plate 5.

The next link, in evidence of the continued dignified shape of the sacred robe, may be seen on Plate 6. The sketch is from the original of Matthew Paris, as instanced by Strutt, who thus explains the subject: "Offa the Second having sent a message " to the Pope for leave to transfer the bishopric of Canterbury " to Lichfield (in his own dominions), Eadulphus is made the " first archbishop."

Dr. Rock supposes the old Norman chasuble of St. Regnobert at Bayeux to be exactly the same as that worn by the Anglo-Saxon priests, and decidedly the type of the earliest continental chasuble. As a confirmation of this, he gives an illustration of the chasuble of St. Thomas of Canterbury, at Sens, borrowed from "Shaw's Dresses and Decorations of the Middle Ages."

This vestment, shown on Plate 7, exhibits a most perfect exemplification of the "flower."

St. Thomas of Canterbury's chasuble is described as 3 feet 10 inches deep; its shape formed from the half of a perfect circle, folded to bring the two even sides together, which were sewn up to the top of the breast, and then sloped gradually round to the back of the neck. So that there should be no other seam but that down the front, and no opening but that to pass the head through. A piece is also cut away at the bottom of the front, diminishing from 2 inches deep at the seam to a mere shaving towards the sides; causing the vestment to be, most properly, somewhat shorter before, than behind.

Owing to the fulness of this robe of circular form, it was necessarily drawn up in folds, when the arms of the wearer were

Plate 5

Fig 1 Fig 2

FROM MOSAICS OF 6TH CENTURY
at Ravenna.

The Chasuble.

raised, from its lower extremity to the shoulders, leaving the surface of the stuff, around and about the neck, comparatively smooth and plain. To our minds, this was the original cause for the vestment being embroidered over the breast and upper part of the back with the ornament called the "flower;" and may also have been the primary reason for the loose pendent orphrey observable in some of the oldest foreign examples of vestment adornment.

It has been suggested that the loose orphrey may have existed apart from the chasuble, for the purpose of being readily shifted or changed. Perhaps so. Still, we cannot resist inclining to the notion that the orphrey was left unattached, save to the upper part of the vestment, that the ornamental work upon it might lose none of its value in effect; while, on the other hand, if fixed to the robe, it would be puckered up when the arms were elevated, and most of its richness concealed.

The orphrey, from "aurifrigium," indicative of beauty and splendour, took the place, as we have already said, of the bands called *clavi*, used for decorating the ordinary dresses of the ancient Romans. And, as thus the *clavus* of the people was in course of time abandoned by the Christian priesthood for the more distinguishing orphrey, so, again, the latter began to take other forms of arrangement on the vestment.

The earliest deviation from the straight band was what we now term the Y cross. And here again was the fitting opportunity for displaying the most elaborate needlework for the perfection of the "flower," within the fork of the Y, as illustrated on Plate 7.

Dr. Rock, in alluding to the Anglo-Saxon chasuble, and "its "curious and richly-embroidered ornament called the 'flower,' " writes so picturesquely about it that we must follow him word for word.

Church Vestments.

He says, "The most beautiful and rarest stuffs were sought after to make this vestment, and often was it ornamented in a way which for some hundreds of years has ceased to be generally followed. This peculiar adornment, or 'flower,' as they called it, consisted of a mass of rich golden needlework, which spread itself in broad thick branches, sometimes before, all over the breast, and always behind upon the higher part of the back and about the shoulders of the chasuble, while all around its neck ran a broad band of gold studded with jewels."

Among Carter's specimens of English Ecclesiastical Costume, published in Fosbroke's "British Monachism," there is a careful sketch from the sculpture of a bishop, exquisitely vested, found in Peterborough Cathedral. The date is supposed to be very early in the twelfth century. The chasuble is adorned with the "flower," rising and expanding from the waist to the collar, in richly embroidered foliage; while down the front is a straight unfigured orphrey, exemplifying the "Tau" or T cross on the breast of the figure. This orphrey being wholly attached to the robe, is partly drawn up with it, owing to the position of the hands, one of which holds the pastoral staff, the other a closed book.

The alb is represented as richly ornamented with a flowing pattern, arranged in vertical bands of some inches deep, up the lower part of the skirt. It is impossible to conceive anything more ecclesiastically chaste and dignified than the apparel of this figure. A representation of it is given on Plate 8.

On the same page, in the above work, Mr. Carter shows the Y cross in an inverted form, on the sacred garment, as discovered on the monument of a priest in Carew Castle, Pembrokeshire, surmising it to be coeval with the before-named effigy. We believe it to be a degree nearer to Anglo-Saxon times than that.

EADULPHUS IS MADE FIRST ARCHBISHOP OF LICHFIELD.

Plate 6

The Chasuble.

From the rigidly plain form of the robes, and the total absence of ornament, excepting the inverted cross, through every portion of them, we presume to date this figure as early as the eleventh century. This will also be found on Plate 8.

Very few examples of the vestment enriched by the beauteous embroidery of the "flower," are to be met with after the close of the twelfth century.

About this period we begin to find the Y cross formed of orphreys of rare needlework; gorgeous in colour, and massive, with inserted plates of gold and silver enamelled. A border of the like work is carried all around the chasuble, and its collar, or orphrey of amice, rendered even more conspicuous, "for "glory and for beauty," than heretofore, by elaborate embroidery, mysteriously wrought to dispute effects of light and shade, with the gold and precious stones, so regally bestowed about it.

Alb, dalmatic, stole, maniple, and cope, are made to match with the Eucharistic robe in luxuriant adornment, and from this time for nearly three centuries, did this splendour in sacerdotal dress continue with unabated brilliancy.

The straight Latin cross on the back of the chasuble did not fully obtain in England till late in the fourteenth century. Then, on its somewhat wide orphreys, figures of saints were worked in a less conventional manner, and holy symbols were also represented in a more literal sense than formerly. Sacred embroidery, too, following closely on the footsteps of drawing and painting, became finer and more studied in execution, as the subjects it was employed upon were brought nearer to Nature, and consequently required more delicate handling for their just development.

Holy and solemn as the Latin cross is in itself, and in other positions, we are bold enough to say that, in a spiritual sense, we

Church Vestments.

consider it less refined, as a figure extending over the vestment, than the more mysterious symbol of the old Y shape.

It is not for us, however, to give examples for the adornment of the chasuble to the exclusion of the plain cross. Highly esteemed and indisputable authorities on the principles of taste in sacred art have shown as much favour to the use of the straight cross on the sacrificial garment as to that of the older form; and we, undoubtedly, shall do our duty best to our readers by assisting them to represent in all ways the unique symbol of our redemption, which can never be too often before our eyes.

This application of the Latin cross may account in a great degree for the curtailment of the ample proportions of the chasuble; for although the front of the vestment had been much lessened in the twelfth century, as instanced on Plate 9, yet the back, as these and other figures show, remained full and uncut for a far longer period; even until the Y cross had begun to fall into disuse.*

One beautiful figure of the fruitfulness of the cross of salvation was at one time represented in a richly embroidered tree, springing from the lowermost border of the deep back of the chasuble, and rearing itself with many spreading branches, over the shoulders, to the collar. This design is occasionally, though not frequently, found on the vestment of the period of transition, particularly abroad, from the Y orphreys to the bold Latin cross.

* The material point in which the Pugin chasuble differs in construction from the more primitive vestment, which it was intended to figure, is in being *cut on the direct cross* of the material, at the shoulders, and joined up afterwards. By this expedient the length of the robe is not curtailed, while its circumference is narrowed, that it may sit about the neck and over the back without folds; an essential circumstance, we own, where the principal adornment of the chasuble is comprised in the form of a large Latin cross.

Plate 7

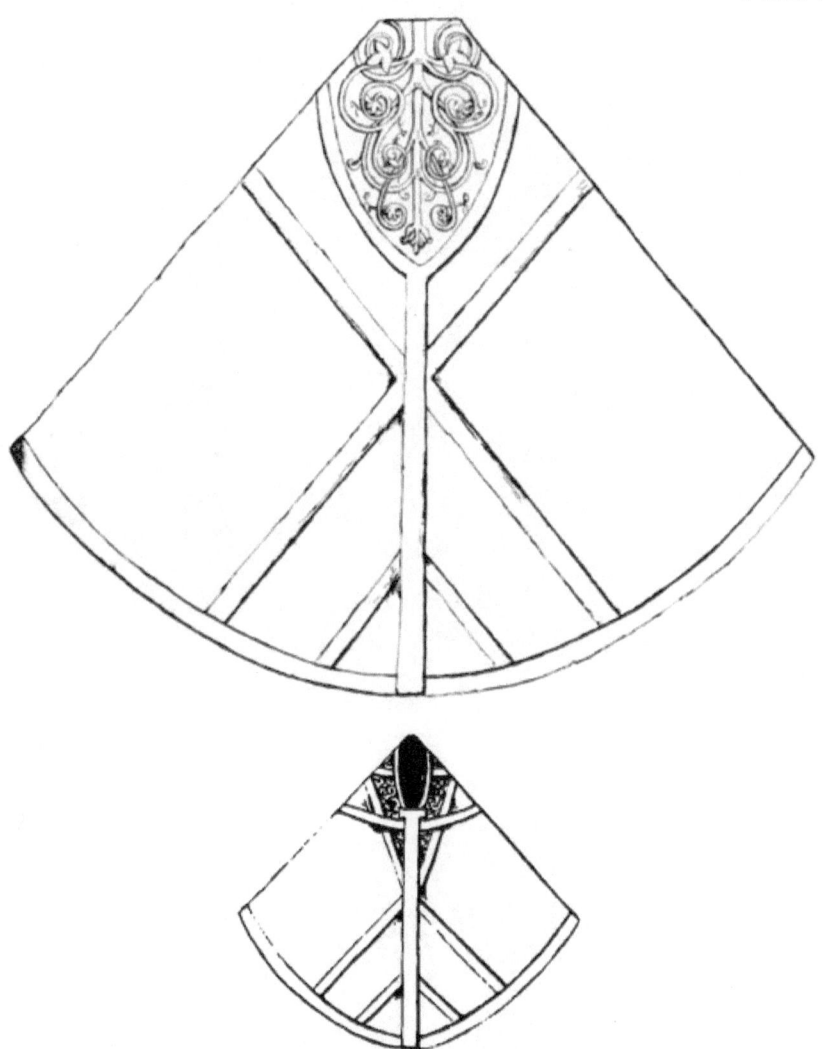

CHASUBLE OF S.^T THOMAS OF CANTERBURY
Preserved at Sens

The Chasuble.

A modern writer has piously and aptly said, speaking of the adornment of the chasuble, with the device which figured the cross as a blossoming tree: "The cross once a mark of shame " is now a symbol of glory, its lifeless arms have blossomed " abundantly and brought forth the fruit of our salvation."

The human representation of the Saviour upon the Cross was not favoured till long after the Lamb had been accepted and used as the type of every Divine attribute of our slain Redeemer. At first, only the sacred bust was introduced, either above or below the cross, on the centre of which was the Agnus Dei. Then the entire figure of our Lord was shown, draped in the long Byzantine robe, by some called the seamless shirt, but not fixed upon the cross. Afterwards, from the twelfth to the fourteenth century, the figure appears as on Plate 10, clothed with a kind of tunic, and nailed by four nails to the cross, but withal, wearing an aspect of dignified majesty and spiritual repose. Finally, the crucified body was portrayed in its most realistic and thrilling form, nailed by three nails to the cross, crowned with thorns, the head depressed, a human expression of agony in the features, and with blood flowing from the wounds.

Whether this positive delineation of the Holy Passion be as solemn, or as dignified, as when symbolized according to the manner affected by the first Christians, is a matter of grave consideration, even of doubt, with many enlightened and right-minded Catholics of our own day.

On Plate 11 we have illustrated a fourteenth-century chasuble, adorned with the Y cross, richly embroidered, after the taste of the time. The figure is sketched from the beautiful brass in the abbey church of St. Albans. It is supposed to be the effigy of the handsome and generous Thomas de la Mare, thirtieth abbat, elected A.D. 1350.

Church Vestments.

Plates 12 and 13, represent the chasuble work of the fifteenth, and, beginning of, the sixteenth centuries. In these examples will be recognized the old Monmouthshire vestment already described, page 18.

Having glanced at the different kinds of needlework adornment bestowed upon the chasuble from its first adoption, by the Christian priesthood, to the sixteenth century, we find one other ornament which we have left yet unmentioned, and which, although not belonging to Embroidery, yet seems to come within our province of observation.

It is the "Rational," a description of large brooch, fastened upon the breast of the chasuble near to the collar, and in most instances which have come before us, worn where no other embellishment appears on the front of the vestment.

On the figure of St. Peter, Plate 8, the rational is distinctly shown. This beautiful statue was sketched for us from the wonderful north porch of Chartres Cathedral, and is, therefore, either of the twelfth or very early in the thirteenth century.

Dr. Rock observes that the "rational" was to be seen as late as the fourteenth century, and "fashioned in all shapes, at one " time round, at another a trefoil or a quatrefoil, but more " generally an oblong square. Seldom was it wrought of any " baser metal than beaten gold, or silver gilt, studded with " precious stones, and as it was worn in imitation, so it had " given to it the name of the Ancient Jewish Rational."

The same learned author has a "rational" in his possession, which was supposed to be the only one known in England, when he published the following account of it in 1849:—

" It is of gilt copper mounted on wood, so as to make it very " light. Its shape a quatrefoil, in each foliation of which " there is, in high relief, a bust of an apostle; in the middle

The Chasuble.

"sits an angel, with the legend 'Matheus.' It seems to have been fastened to the chasuble by means of a long pin like a brooch. Its date is early in the thirteenth century; and it measures six inches in length, by just as many in breadth, and is three-quarters of an inch in thickness. The custom of wearing the 'rational' lasted, it would seem, longer on the Continent than here, and proofs of its use, even until a late period, may be traced in France and the Low Countries."

Thus far, all the illustrations we have given of the chasuble, and its enriching accessories, are, with the trifling variations we have named, in strict accordance with the ancient typical form; and, therefore, as meet for imitation in the Catholic ritual of to-day, as they were twelve hundred years ago.

On Plate 14 is exhibited a fac-simile of the holy vestment at Aix-la-Chapelle, carefully sketched from the original copy of which Dr. Rock possessed himself. The crosses and circles, which comprise its decoration, are formed of pearls, and have a most chaste effect on the violet silk ground. We have selected this, under authority, as a standard for the correct shape, embodying, as it does, much of the dignity of the round primitive chasuble, without its cumbersomeness, and enough of the old Gothic sacred character to prove its identity with the chasuble of remote Christian times, when, what is learning now, was pious inspiration, and the priestly mission was fulfilled in every way as though it came direct from God.

The vestment figured on Plate 12, is, as we have said, page 19, of the Italian shape, which at this moment is more favoured in Rome than that of the fine old Gothic model.

We are willing to bow with deference to the high authority by whom these vestments are sanctioned; but, at the same time, our belief in the beauty of the ancient form remains unshaken.

Church Vestments.

The miserable shape of the vestment of the present century, in France, has only to be seen, by the lover of orthodox things, to be avoided. It usually takes the wretched form given in outline on Plate 15, and is either ornamented with needlework of meagre, half secular, half sacred designs, unmeaning as they are unimpressive, or with tawdry orphreys, woven of a spare surface of silk on thick cotton foundations, which are laid on the vestment with borderings of tinsel lace. Then, with buckram between, and a lining of glazed calico, the chasuble is made up to hang over the figure of the priest in a commonplace and undignified manner, calculated to excite in the minds of all, save the truly pious Catholic, more ridicule than reverence.

How to account for this absence in France of the right spirit for guidance in ecclesiastical decoration, we are nearly at a loss. That it once existed there to an inspired degree, will be undeniable, so long as such cathedrals as Abbeville, Amiens, Chartres, Rouen, and a full score more equally fine, have one stone left upon another to meet the sceptic's eye. It is nevertheless true of the present, that greatly as our neighbours exceed all other nations in refined taste, when exercised on secular objects, they have no speciality for the adornment of sacerdotal or other Church appointments.

The first French Revolution, which for the time overthrew all Christian, for Pagan, institutions, undoubtedly did its work of perversion within as without the Church, and most likely helped to cast into the cold shade the beautiful traditions of the primitive faith, which have given to everything used in the solemn service of God a holy and figurative signification.

Within the last few years, however, we have had occasion to note here and there in France that vestments of a better style are gradually being brought again into use; a revival which we

Plate 8

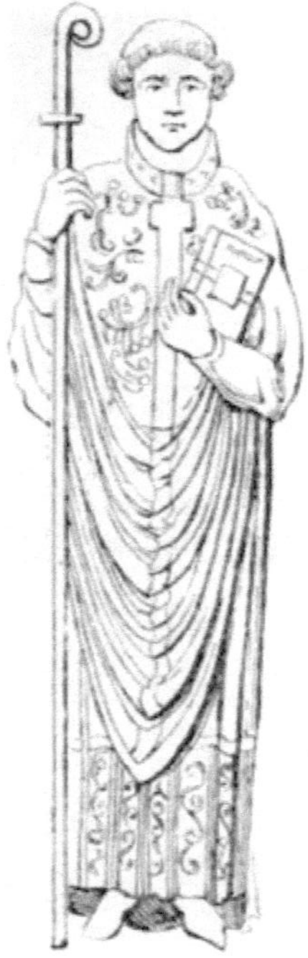

12 Cent.

St PETER FROM CHARTRES

Early in 13th Century

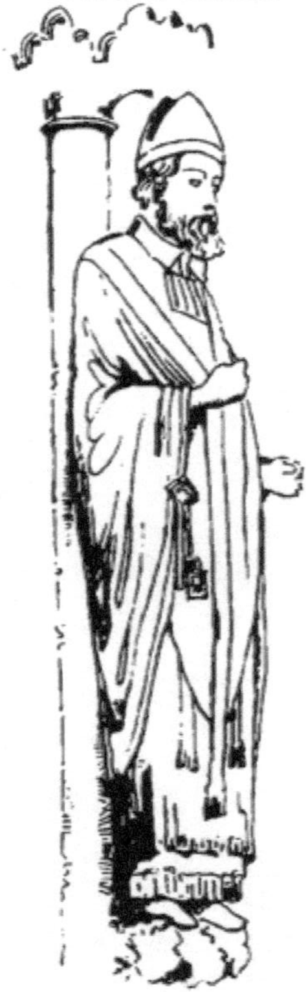

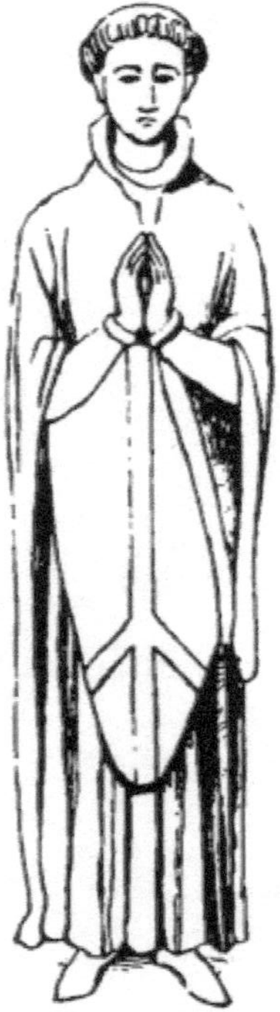

[illegible] Cent.

ardently desire to see general throughout a country so singularly favoured by ancient examples of appropriate beauty in Church work.

We have hinted that it is not our intention to write at large upon foreign vestments. The two kinds we have touched upon are so frequently and indiscriminately made, and given by persons of probably greater piety than taste, in sacred art, to English priests, that we have deemed it incumbent upon us to point out their want of affinity with the original type of the sacrificial garment, which has been so fully recognised here for the last twenty-five years.

VARIOUS WAYS OF ORNAMENTING THE CHASUBLE.
THE " FLOWER."

The first, and undoubtedly the finest, of the old examples for the adornment of the sacred robe in needlework is that of the " flower," for which we present on Plate 16, two designs, to be embroidered either in real gold or rich gold silk. We marvel that this beautiful ornament has not received as much notice from other writers on the revival of sacred vestiary splendour, excepting Canon Rock, as we are disposed to give it.

The costliness of its production has been urged as an excuse for its non-adoption. We cannot give in our adhesion to this; for although the " flower," as worked on the vestment of St. Thomas of Canterbury, was often of naught else but massive gold embroidery, yet the chasuble of St. Dunstan, figured and described in the " Church of our Fathers," from an Anglo-Saxon MS., was wrought with the "flower" in *red* needlework only; and the Saint, who during his life gave so much aid to sacerdotal ornament, even by drawing and making designs for it himself,

Church Vestments.

would surely not have been represented, as bearing upon his own episcopal dress any decoration which was unorthodox, or less rich than his compeers in the Church would wear.

A great deal of work is comprised in the "flower," for it should be of a luxuriant pattern, but not more than, or as much as, would be spread over the surface of needlework orphreys, which, *vide* Plate 17, may be very consistently left without ornament, where the "flower" is shown.

The Y cross of a chasuble embroidered with the "flower" in gold, may be formed of cloth of gold, edged with a narrow woven lace of a mixture of gold and the colour of the vestment; or it may be either of satin or velvet, of the same hue as the garment, and edged with a narrow gold lace.

The "flower" should present the appearance of having been wrought upon the actual vestment, although, for the convenience of the embroiderer, it may be worked upon a separate piece of silk, and laid down upon the shape of the chasuble afterwards; as the humeral, or shoulder orphreys will be placed over, and conceal, the division necessarily made in the silk. The same method may be pursued with the embroidery upon the breast, where, as at the back, the orphreys will cover the join.

Supposing it to be deemed necessary to work the "flower" in crimson on a white vestment, the orphreys should be of crimson, and edged with a gold lace to correspond with the embroidery, which should be slightly raised by string, as directed in " Church " Embroidery," and edged with gold " pearl-purl."

Only scrollage of the particular character exhibited on Plate 7, can properly represent the grace of the "flower." Our designs will be recognised as simple imitations of the old examples of the ornament, which can neither be improved upon in sacred refinement, nor augmented in richness of effect.

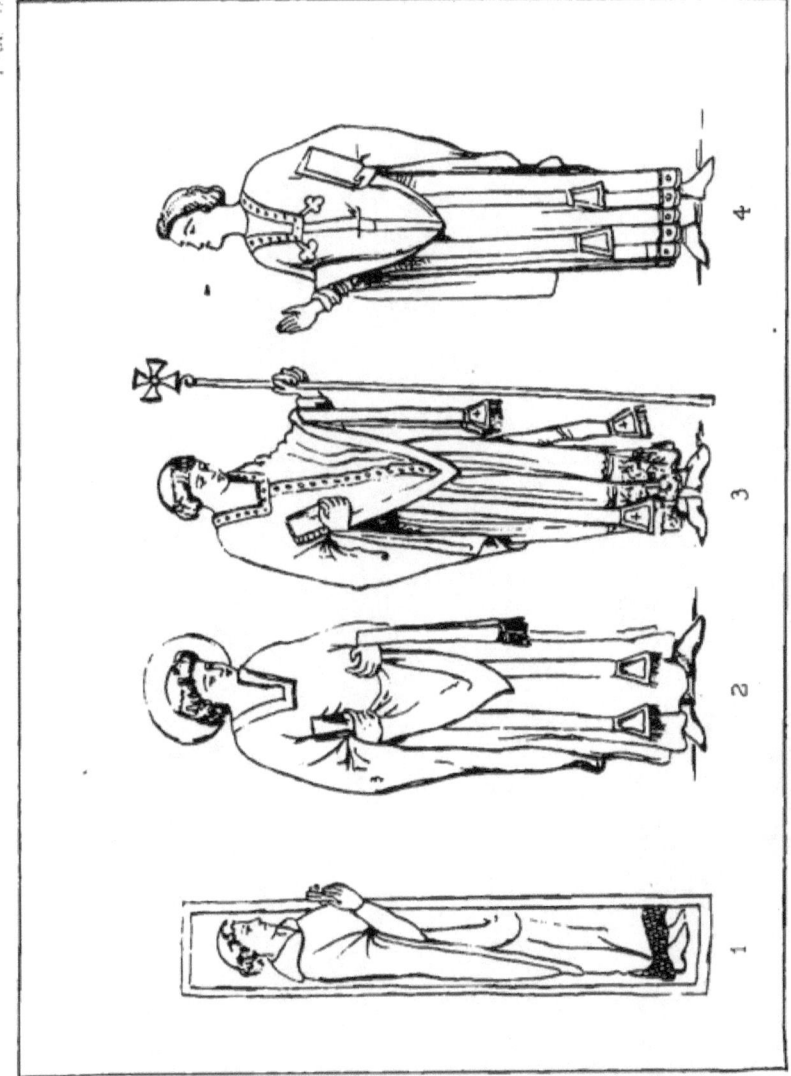

VESTED PRIESTS OF 12TH & 13TH CENTURIES

The "Flower."

We do not show separate patterns for the work on the breast of the chasuble, since it will be necessary only to take away a portion of the device from the upper part of the back, to leave the opening to pass the head through, to perfect the pattern for the front. By reference to Plate 7, this expedient may be clearly comprehended.

To adorn the breast of the chasuble as well as the back with the "flower" is not imperative; but, as a rule, the *orphrey* should correspond on both sides of the chasuble, should meet at the same angle on the shoulders, and diverge into the single vertical band at the centre of the breast, as upon the middle of the back.

In ancient times the orphreys were called thus: the front vertical band, the *pectoral;* the corresponding one behind, the *dorsal;* and those which extended to the shoulders, the *humerals*.

Where the "flower" is embroidered upon the vestment, and the orphreys are unfigured, a needlework border around the chasuble is a worthy ornamentation. Further on, we will give simple borders for this purpose. Their execution will amply repay the worker who is bent upon enriching the chasuble to her utmost. These narrow borders, to be quite correct, should be embroidered actually upon the vestment, and it is impossible to execute them well out of a frame. The only right way to frame such work is the following :—

The vestment is to be cut to its right shape, and the pattern of the border drawn upon it. Then a piece of fine firm linen of even sides is to be tightly framed, and a portion of the silk embracing the pattern of the border tacked upon it. When as much as can be conveniently embroidered on this piece of linen is accomplished, it should be cut out of the frame, and another piece of linen inserted, and so on, until the whole border is worked.

It is, now, the almost invariable custom to bind the chasuble

Church Vestments.

all round with an inch lace harmonizing in colour and pattern with the wider lace of which the orphreys are frequently made, or with the shades most prominent in the embroidered decorations of the robe. This fashion, like that of using machine-made orphreys instead of those wrought by the hand, is not to be condemned. A narrow border of needlework around the vestment will greatly enhance its beauty and its grace; but it is better to employ an edge of woven lace than to slight or impoverish the embellishment of the more important parts of the sacred garment, that time and materials may be saved for an embroidered binding. A well-made fringe of an inch and a quarter deep, embracing the principal colours used in the embroidery on the chasuble, and placed against the edging of lace or needlework, is in correct taste, and will add greatly to the enrichment of the vestment.

The width of the Y orphrey may vary from three and a half to five inches, the edging inclusive, to be regulated according to the richness of the pattern forming the "flower;" for it must be borne in mind that a slight flowing design would be, very improperly, cast into shade by wide bands of a definite colour encompassing it about, and *vice versâ*.

This hint belongs to the principles of good taste, which, in subjects like the present, are more often outraged from want of thought than from errors of judgment.

Plain orphreys of five inches and less should be attached to the chasuble by an edge of woven lace, commencing at half an inch, but never exceeding three-quarters of an inch in width.

The Y Cross.

On Plate 17, we show the Cross enriched, at the junction of its plain orphreys, by a conventional drawing of the Lamb

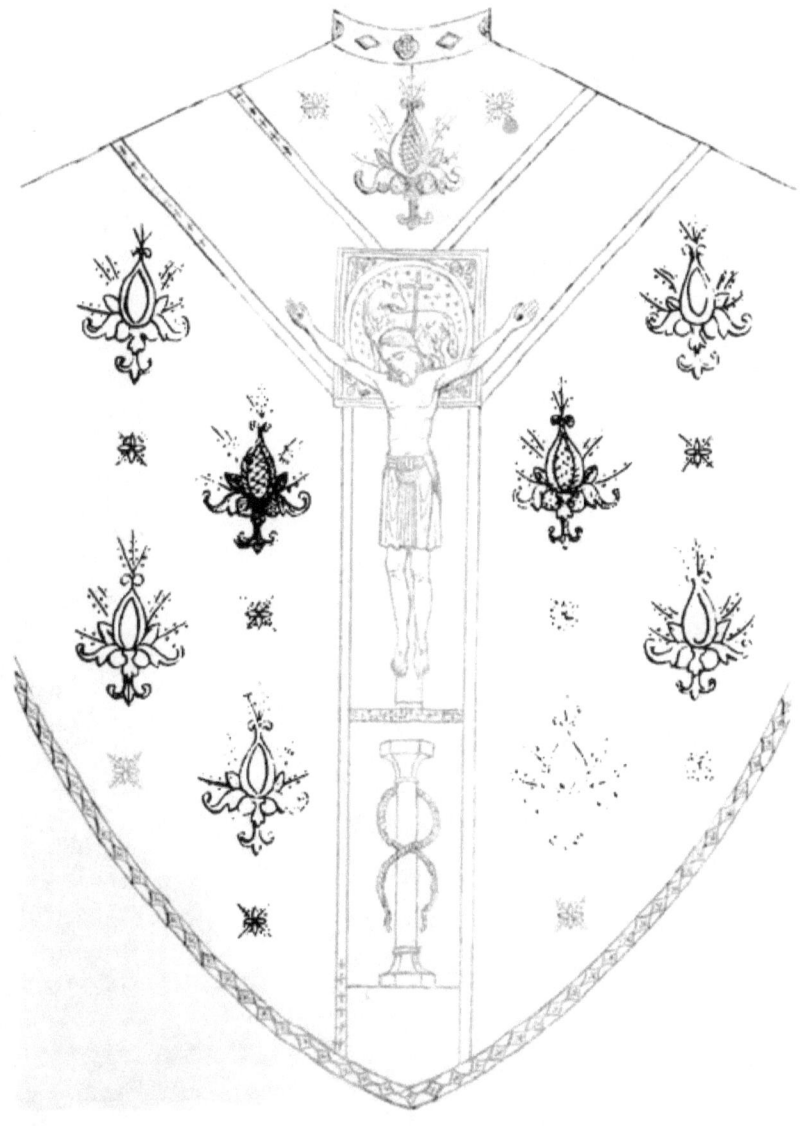

Plate 10.

The Y Cross.

of God, taken from an example in sculpture of the tenth century.

No more exquisite effect of chaste colouring can be conceived than this simple arrangement of ornament on the chasuble suggests.

The vestment should be white; the orphreys, cloth of gold, woven with the faintest indication of a crimson tracery on its surface. The Lamb to be embroidered in silver, or in pure white silk shaded to a pearly grey. Its background a clear, heavenly blue, diapered by gold tambour thread. Circle of nimbus, couched in gold. Crosses, white, on a blood-red ground. Cross borne by Lamb, gold.

Ground of band, describing geometrical figure, gold. Letters, "Ecce Agnus Dei," silver, edged with dark violet.

Tracery ornament on cuspated divisions of geometrical figure, dull-red silk. "I. H. S.," crimson, edged with silver. Ornament on each side of "I. H. S.," silver. Narrow border of cross, and edging of chasuble, embroidery, in gold and dull red.

The front orphreys to be formed precisely like the back, but with the omission of the design from the centre.

The lining to be plain gold-colour silk, or a mixture of crimson and gold.

The next example of the Y cross, Plate 10, exhibits the crucified Saviour from an authority which dates as early as the twelfth century. The figure is that referred to page 53, as fixed to the cross by four nails, and vested in a kind of tunic.

Six refined shades of flesh-colour will be required for the figure of our Lord, and four shades of golden brown for the hair. Three shades of grey, with white, should be used for the tunic, and a dull crimson, striped with gold passing, for the girdle.

Church Vestments.

The nails may be shown by a dark-slate shade. The pillar to be two shades of light, and one of dark, *warm* stone colour. The cords, dark drab, with a much darker shade to mark the twist. The worker may not require reminding that too much attention cannot be bestowed on the treatment of this most sacred figure. It is to such subjects as this that our remarks on page 17 of " Church Embroidery" directly apply.

The figure, also the pillar and cords, should be worked upon linen, and transferred afterwards to the cross. The edging of the Y orphrey is to be couched in crimson silk, as a ground to the small crosses, which are to be laid upon it, formed of two lines of gold " passing," sewn down with orange. The Y orphrey may be either of cloth of gold, as described for vestment on Plate 17, or it may be of gold, couched quite flat, or in a raised stitch.

The larger powdering figures on this vestment are to be worked as follows:—

Large scroll leaves, springing from lower part of pine, two shades of lilac veined with " passing."

Small leaves above scrolls, dull crimson.

Stem of sprig, rich gold-colour twist silk, couched one thread at a time with copper brown.

Inside of pine, lilac chequered with " passing," stitched down with lilac sewings of a darker shade.

Outside of pine, very light copper brown, worked in Berlin silk.

Diverging sprays, orange floss, enriched by " passing," and spangles.

Small powdering figures, gold, sewn down with dull crimson, with orange sprays, enriched by spangles.

Edging of chasuble, lilac and dull red, alternated, worked as a

Plate II

THOMAS DE LA MARE 30th ABBOT OF ST ALBAN'S

Orphreys.

tracery, and edged with one line of coarse gold "passing." Figure in centre of each diamond, gold thread.

This design has been arranged for the green vestment to be worn on ordinary Sundays and Ferias. The lining is to be either green, dull red, or gold.

The front of the chasuble is to be powdered with sprigs the same as the back, and may have a plain straight orphrey up the centre, or no orphrey at all, according to taste or circumstances.

Orphreys of Woven Lace.

In lieu of needlework, orphreys of woven lace are frequently used.

During the last twenty-five years the manufacture of this particular *Church* lace, as it is called, has been brought to great perfection. The most finished patterns of any number of colours are now produced in the loom with such beauty of effect, that many of them, at a distance of twenty yards, might well pass for embroidery. Those of English designs and fabrication are the best, but these are not all of one quality. The inferior kinds are very flimsy, and apt to be flossy and wear badly, and are little better than ordinary Orris lace, which the foreign Church laces so greatly resemble. The firmness or substance of the English lace is, like the cost, increased with the number of colours used in the pattern.*

We do not advocate the use of any kind of lace for the adornment of the chasuble in preference to needlework, which we consider should never be abandoned while adequate time and means may be found for its accomplishment.

---

* A very good lace of cloth of gold is to be had of the regulation width for orphreys. We have seen some beautiful specimens at Mr. Helbronner's, 265, Regent Street.

Church Vestments.

THE LATIN CROSS.

We have so many fine examples, in ancient needlework, still preserved to us, of the custom of adorning the Latin cross of the vestment of the fourteenth and fifteenth centuries with figures of our Lord and the blessed Saints and Angels, that we dare not presume to offer any suggestions of our own on this class of sacred embroidery. All true lovers of the art, who are not already familiar with specimens of this wonderful branch of it, may at once be made so by referring to Plates 12 and 13, upon which the beautiful Monmouthshire vestment is shown; and for further enlightenment we recommend them to the South Kensington Museum, where whole weeks may be spent as moments in acquiring a knowledge for the painting of sacred subjects in silks and gold, from those archangels and angels with their attributes, and saints and martyrs with their symbols, which are all to be found there on the sacerdotal garments of the above-named period, graphically represented by the aid of the needle alone; and with a holy feeling, and a sublimity, which we moderns cannot imitate too closely.

To Dr. Rock we are indebted for the following richly-expressed summary of the ancient embroideries collected at the Great Exhibition of 1862 :—

" With regard to the subjects figured in these ecclesiastical
" embroideries, we may see, at a glance, that the one untiring
" wish of the designer, whatever be the period of their execution,
" was to set before the people's eyes and bring to mind, strongly
" and unmistakably, the grand doctrine of the Atonement.
" Whether it be cope, or chasuble, or reredos, or altar frontal,
" this teaching is put forth upon it.

" Beginning with the Incarnation, sometimes we have shown
" us Gabriel speaking his message to the Blessed Virgin Mary,

Plate 12.

BACK OF ANCIENT VESTMENT

The Latin Cross.

"with the three-flowered lily standing between them; or the
"Nativity, with the shepherds or the wise men kneeling in
"adoration, acknowledging the divinity of our Lord even as a
"new-born child; then some passage from His Passion; His
"scourging at the pillar or the bearing of His cross, or His being
"crowned with thorns; always His crucifixion; often, above, His
upraised person like a king enthroned, and crowning her of
' whom He took flesh; while everywhere about the vestment are
"figured apostles, martyrs, and saints, all nimbed with glory, and
"among winged seraphim standing upon wheels, thus signifying
"that heaven is thrown open to fallen but redeemed man, who
"by the atonement wrought for him by our divine Redeemer,
"is made the fellow-companion of angels and cherubim."

Some knowledge of the way of executing the lovely stitchery, so bounteously bestowed on much of the work thus described, may be acquired by studying our instructions in the chapter on *stitches* in "Church Embroidery."

Upon the decorated Latin cross, Plate 18, we have not been able to forbear giving a design for the centre, wherein is introduced the figure of our Lord seated, from Queen Mary's Psalter, and attended by angels, sketched from the Adoration of the Blessed Virgin on the glorious tympanum of the western door of Wells Cathedral.

The ground of this vestment is to be cloth of gold, or a very rich silk of the old cream-coloured tint; the former material should be chosen if possible. The cross is to be a mass of needlework, wrought upon stout linen, and transferred to the chasuble afterwards. The figure of the Saviour, with the vesica encompassing it, should be embroidered separately, and attached to its place upon the cross after the rest of the work is completed. The angels to be treated in like manner.

Church Vestments.

A pale celestial *blue* is to be the groundwork of the cross. It is to be of floss silk, and couched one thread at a time with fine white sewing silk.

The groundwork of the legend is to be worked in *long stitch* in fine floss, which is to be deep red under the letters, and two shades paler under the tracery.

Letters, gold, edged by a fine line of black.

Tracery, gold.

Stars, gold, edged with black.

Angels' albs, fine, pure white floss, shaded with soft grey.

Wings of angels, radiant with many colours towards the tips, and streaked with gold and silver; but fading into the softest white at the top, and about the shoulders.

Hair of angels, golden orange.

Very delicate flesh tints for the faces and hands.

Description of figure of our Lord :—

Inner robe, gold.

Outer robe, rich red.

Nimbus, red upon gold.

Hair, rich brown.

Throne and footstool, gold, shaded with brown silk.

Distant background, within vesica, deep cerulean blue, couched with sewing silk a shade lighter.

Background of throne, gold, couched with orange.

Band of vesica, *basket-stitch* in gold, sewn with orange, over four rows of fine string.

Orb held by the Saviour, gold; horizontal and upright lines to be silver, edged with black.

The crowns at each extremity of the cross may, or may not be worked; they do not belong to the work of the middle ages, as in every instance we find the cross on the chasuble without

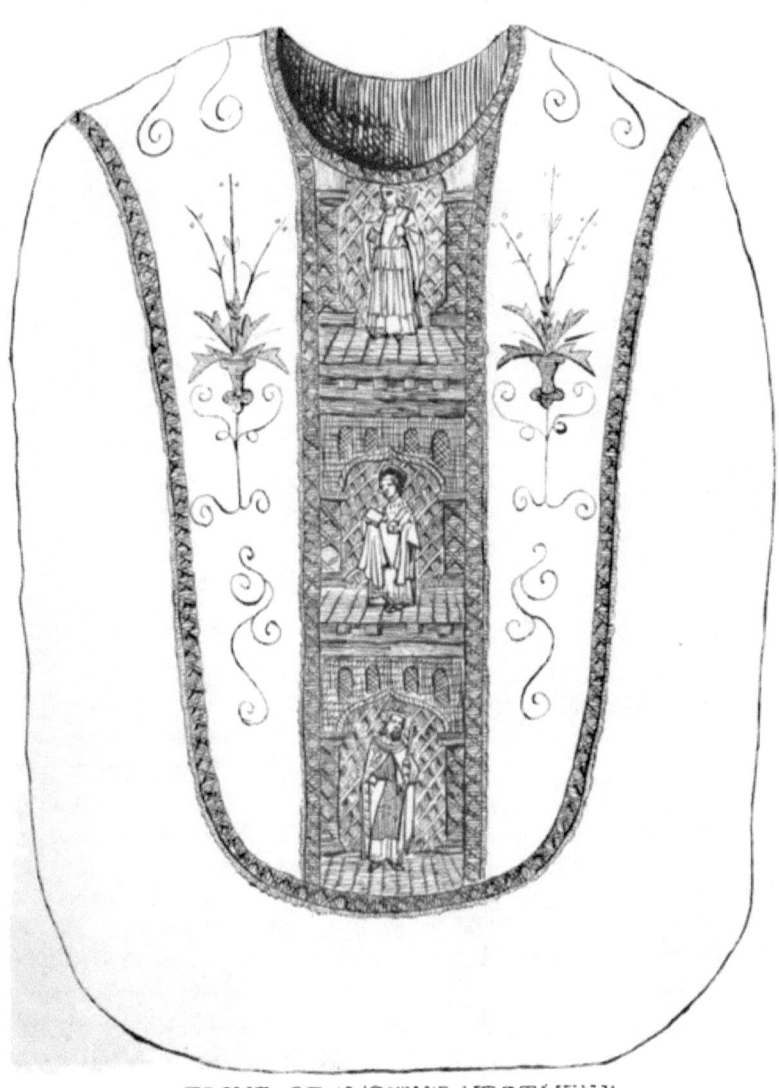

FRONT OF ANCIENT VESTMENT

The Lily Chasuble.

florid terminations of any kind. Crowns and foliated finials are quite of recent adoption. Sometimes, only the three upper crowns are used, and sometimes only the two arms of the cross are thus treated, in which case the stem of the cross reaches the upper and lower extremities of the vestment.

Those of our cross are to be wrought only in gold, and outlined with dark red. The outline border of the cross will be best in gold *basket-stitch* over four rows of string stitched down with red.

The lining of this chasuble may be of gold, crimson, or of white silk.

CHASUBLE TO BE WORN ON FESTIVALS OF THE BLESSED VIRGIN; BUT ESPECIALLY DESIGNED FOR THE ANNUNCIATION.

Innumerable are the groups of sacred figures which, through all Christian ages, have been designed to illustrate, in needlework, different edifying passages in the sanctified life of our Lady.

From the Annunciation, as quoted page 64, to her death, the pious believers of the past have loved to represent the mother of the Saviour in every phase of her blessed career, accompanied at all times by the highest attributes of womanly virtue and holiness, figuratively and spiritually expressed.

So many of these devoutly inspired works are still extant, and generally accessible, and so few of them can be exceeded in decorous and refined treatment, that we shrink from either repeating any of these already often-repeated subjects, or from giving imitations of them, whose only originality might be their only imperfection.

Church Vestments.

As apart from figure subjects, those of flowers suitably conventionalized are capable of the sweetest expression of lofty sentiment in a symbolic form, while affording unlimited scope for richness of effect and for variation in stitchery, we have taken the lily, choice emblem of the purity of the Blessed Virgin, wherewith to embellish the vestment to be worn in her honour. See Plate 19.

This chasuble should be made of a rich white silk, and lined with gold colour.

The monogram, gold bullion.

Lilies, gold, or gold silk.

Leaves, two delicate shades of apple green, veined with gold.

All the stems, the lightest shade of apple green.

Bulbs of lilies, two soft shades of sea-green silk; the darkest shade to be worked nearest to the stem.

Stamens, gold thread, terminated by a small gold bead.

The form of the Latin cross is to be represented simply by the narrow border of embroidery, which is to be one inch wide, and worked in celestial blue Berlin silk, held down by diagonal stitches of gold passing, couched with orange, and dotted between with seed pearls.

Border edging the garment, to be worked in the same manner.

Fleur-de-lis, powdering the vestment, to be of white Berlin silk, finely couched with celestial blue, and edged with gold "passing," sewn down with orange. Bands across fleur-de-lis, "passing," raised over two rows of fine string.

We now proceed to remark upon the

Different Materials of which a Chasuble may, and may not, be made.

Velvets, satins, and silks, either figured or plain, and cloths of gold and of silver, are the only textiles proper for the sacrificial

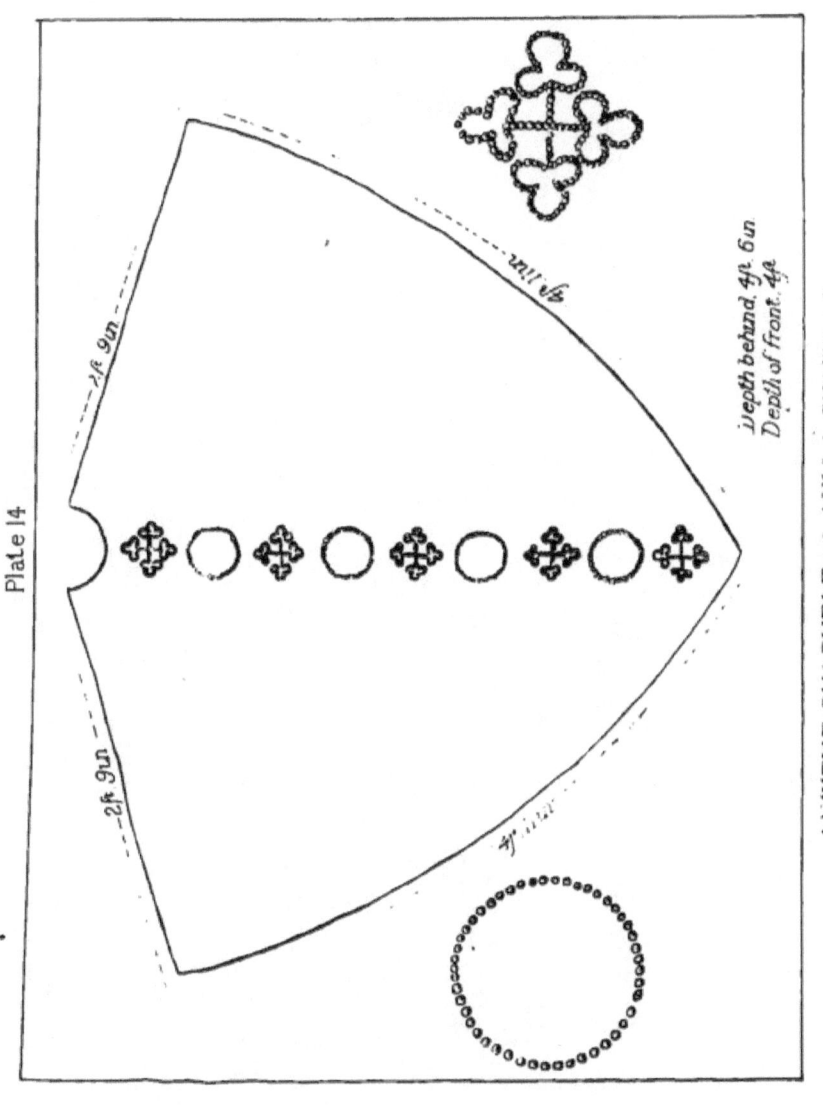

ANCIENT CHASUBLE at AIX-LA-CHAPELLE.
From a copy taken by Dr Rock

Materials for Chasubles.

robe, which should also invariably be lined with silk, be it of ever so thin a quality, in preference to either cotton or woollen materials of any description.

Fabrics of rich but soft texture should be especially chosen for the chasuble, which, as we have already endeavoured to show, should enfold the priest with the grace of simplicity, as on fig. 1, Plate 8, or should invest the wearer with dignified grandeur, as illustrated on Plate 11.

Neither of these desirable effects can be produced from commonplace stiff materials; such, in fact, as are usually but a mixture of badly-prepared silk and inferior cotton, wherein the latter predominates most unfairly. On the other hand, there is an evil to be guarded against, viz., the use of silks of really genuine quality, but of so ductile a make that they are apt to cling about the figure meanly and flimsily, instead of enveloping it in the full massive folds which should dignify and distinguish the chasuble for its lofty purpose.

Some Ritualistic clergymen, in their adoption lately of the sacred vestment, have favoured its construction from plain silks, or from damasks of the lightest and softest fabrication, assigning their preference, first, to a determination to copy rigidly only the earliest examples of silk foundations used in sacerdotal dress; and, secondly, to the necessity for keeping the priest during the solemn performance of his office as little as possible encumbered by his robes.

The first of these reasons opens up a wide and vague field for research, and one likely to prove in the end too unproductive for our sphere of action. Nevertheless, we believe the period to be not only very remote, but obscure, from which authorities have been obtained for some of the poor-looking sarsenet-like vestments of sombre shades which we have occasionally of late been

Church Vestments.

called upon to see. The second reason has to do with individual notions of convenience, such as, so we have been taught, the devoted minister of the altar, unless enfeebled by age or weakly from illness, never allows himself to entertain.

Could we possibly obtain clear proofs of the precise nature of the productions of the silk loom for the Church, when the very art itself of weaving silk was new in England, we should not for an instant entertain the thought that silks of this description only were correct for Ecclesiastical use.

The same argument which has been urged against the practice of following in precise detail the crude drawings in Christian art of the ancients will apply to the textile manufactures of primitive times, when we may be sure that the weaver, like the artist and embroiderer, used all the knowledge the age afforded him to perfect his work, and the more especially that which he was privileged to produce for the service of God in His Church.*

The brocaded silks, and the "bawdkin," so often referred to in old records of sacerdotal adornment, must have been remarkable for their firm, though soft texture; otherwise, those heavy embroideries, with enamels and gold and silver plates, studded with pearls and precious stones, by which, we are told, the chasuble was enriched, could never have been supported upon them.

Solitary instances of what has been fitly termed exaggerated richness are recorded of some of the vestments of mediæval

---

* "As in the old law so in the new, the ministering garments of the priesthood have been "of the best that might be, often of very precious stuffs, always seemly; the mosaics of "Ravenna alone are witnesses to this in the sixth century, while the later curious 'Liber "Pontificalis' particularizes in one place the hangings for the altar, palergium chrysoclavum "preciossissimum, coöpertorium purpureum cum cruce; in another, the 'vestis holoserica "vestis auro texta habens historiam Salvatoris et Apostolos,' and other rich liturgical "requisites, brought by the faithful as their offerings at the shrine of the apostles in Rome."
—Dr. Rock.

Materials for Chasubles.

times, such as was the case in the twelfth century with one, at least, of the chasubles belonging to the cathedral at Mentz, which was so weighted with splendour that the celebrant was compelled to exchange it at the offertory for a lighter vestment. This mistaken excess in sacerdotal adornment rarely, if ever, occurred in England, where, with few exceptions, before the sixteenth century, we meet with no sacred decoration which does not, in a great measure, "owe its chief beauty to its propriety."

That heavy gold embroidery raised and tortured into smoothness, till it looks like wood-carving gilt, which within the last half-century we have too often seen on the robes of priests ministering at English altars, has been wrought abroad, principally in France and Belgium. It is usually seen mounted on the shape depicted Plate 15, with which it has a true affinity. And so we dismiss it, for it is wholly without the grace of sacred needlework.

Figured silks, if employed for the chasuble, should be of small and unobtrusive patterns, particularly if the orphreys be of embroidery.

A *powdering*, *i.e.*, detached figures placed at regular intervals, is better than a connected overspreading design called a *diapering*, and whether it be woven in the loom, or wrought by the needle, will greatly augment the beauty of an embroidered orphrey, as *see* Plate 10.

There are few silks which, in the making up for vestments, are not improved by a lining of thin unbleached calico being placed between themselves and the inner silk lining. Of this, we will write more fully further on.

Velvet, although for every purpose considered the richest of all textile materials, scarcely excepting cloth of gold, yet need not be esteemed essentially the best for the vestment. A velvet chasuble suitably ornamented, of the correct ample shape, and no

Church Vestments.

other should be sanctioned, is liable to look more costly than chaste, and more ponderous than graceful. Where a good silk will gather up in rich folds with the action of the arms, velvet will draw up stiffly in pleats, and rest upon rather than envelop the person.

Those truly beautiful velvets, woven in colours, upon which so many of the sacred embroideries in the South Kensington Museum are to be found, are North Italian, and most of them of the fifteenth century.

No modern fabrication, with the like pretence to richness, could have exceeded these velvets when they first left the loom. Some of them are woven in large patterns which are literally weighty to look upon with gold thread; but from the excellence of the well-spun silk, and the purity, and consequent suppleness of the metal, the whole fabric is softer, and more inclined to fall in graceful folds, than many of our brocaded silks.

For copes, tunicles, etc., nothing can surpass the worth of velvet, but, for the reasons we have named, it is certainly less desirable for the sacrificial vestment.

Orphreys of velvet for silk vestments are unexceptionable, the very purpose of the orphrey being fully answered by the superiority of its material to that which it is intended to beautify.

Satin orphreys are also very seemly on silks of dark surfaces. Not long since, we were shown a chasuble of soft, thick, white silk, enriched by Y shaped orphreys of a glowing gold-colour satin. It was entirely without embroidery, but the effect was chaste as it was unique, and in every respect orthodox. The satin was of the richest quality, and therefore likely to retain its beauty simultaneously with the silk upon which it was laid; for a good satin will neither crease by folding, nor lose its gloss by wear.

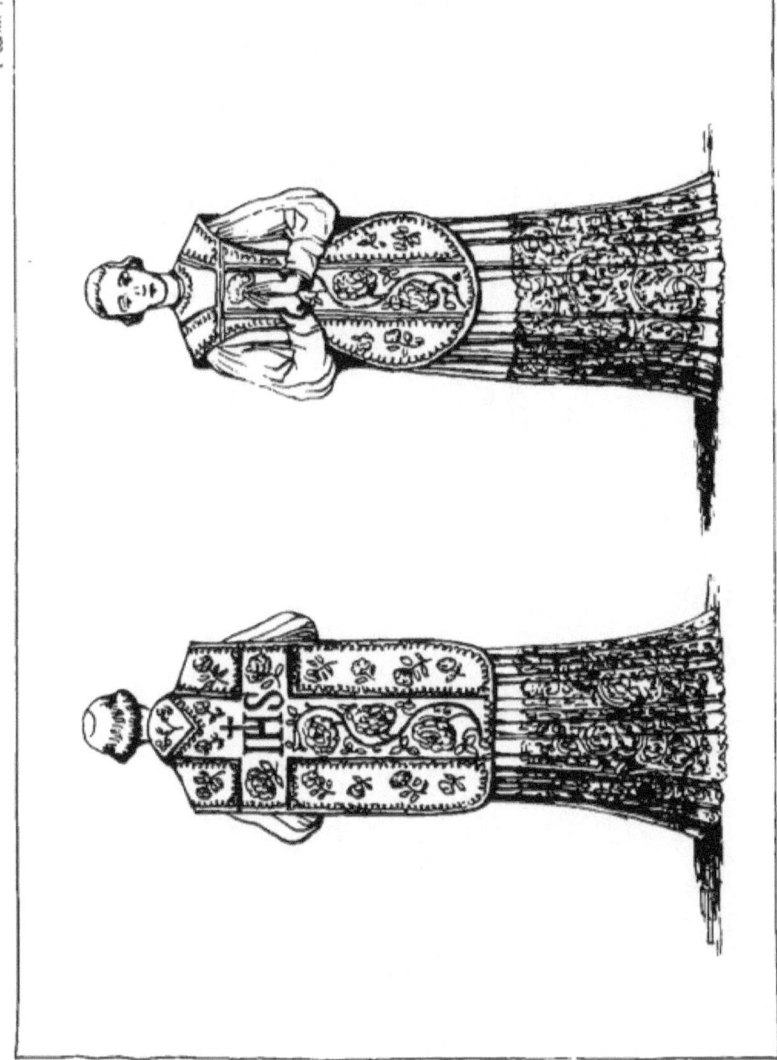

THE INCORRECT CHASUBLE.

Materials for Chasubles.

Silks of white ground woven with coloured flowers, are not correct for a vestment which is to have variegated needlework on its orphreys. For such silks the orphreys should be of plain material, velvet or otherwise; and if embroidered, principally with gold or silver.

Cloth of gold orphreys are superb upon any fabric, and, like satin, will embellish the chasuble suitably where needlework is unattainable.

Merino, alpaca, or any woollen, not to say inferior, material whatever, should not be thought of, as fitted for the robe which " for glory and for beauty " should exceed all others.

In these days, a minister, however zealous, may be unable to impress the whole of his congregation at once with the belief that a special garment should be consecrated for the office of the Holy Eucharist; but among those who are with him in the desire to revive the glories of the Christian ritual, there should be as little difficulty found in raising 10*l.* for the furtherance of an object, deemed essential to the service of God, as 10*s.* for the need of man.

It must be a slight privation indeed which an individual, with the smallest means, has to endure for the sake of the mite offered among many, for the purchase of a chasuble worthy of the motive which calls for it.

It is not yet, neither can we suppose that it will ever be, upon record, that any one was ruined by giving freely in the name of the Lord; and we still hope to see the day when we may no longer have to read in Church papers repeated appeals from the same clergyman for sums wherewith to buy vestments—sums which scandalize us by their insignificance; each being often less than a middle-class wife or daughter will spend on her second-best gown.

Church Vestments.

VI.

GENERAL DIRECTIONS FOR MAKING UP VESTMENTS.

ALL vestments, from the chasuble to the cope, should be made up with an inner lining between the outside material and the silk lining.

Unbleached calico of a tolerable substance should be used for this purpose when the silk of the vestment is of a medium quality, but if the outer fabric be very stout or rich, the inner lining may be less firm.* This layer of calico should be cut with great precision to the size and shape which the vestment is to be when made, and then tacked evenly upon the superior or upper silk; which, if it be for a chasuble that is embroidered round the edge, must have three-quarters of an inch of silk left beyond the needlework, to be turned over upon the calico.

The silk lining must also be left with an ample turning, to be neatly felled down upon its own side.

If the vestment is to have a flat lace binding, or a fringe, or both, the superior silk should be cut away to the exact edge of the calico foundation, while the silk lining should still be left with three-quarters of an inch of silk beyond the edge to be turned over and tacked down upon the surface of the upper material. Upon this, the flat lace binding is to be laid. If a fringe is to go beyond, the binding should not be brought to the extreme

---

* A good jaconet muslin will be found the most suitable inner lining for such fabrics.

DESIGNS FOR THE "FLOWER".

How to make Vestments.

edge of the garment, but a space should be left corresponding with the width of the heading of the fringe, to give the latter firmness and support.

This method of turning the silk lining over upon the surface of the superior material should always be adopted for vestments with woven lace bindings or fringes. It is advisable, not only on the principle of neatness, but on that of saving, as not a shred of the upper silk need be left beyond the edge of the calico foundation by this plan; and where the material of the garment is costly, or, as it sometimes is, scarce, even inches may thus be taken into consideration at a great advantage.

The chalice-veil, stole, and in short, all the principal articles of sacerdotal dress, accordingly as they have, or have not, lace bindings, should be made up upon either one or the other of the principles above named, and never without an inner lining, be it ever so thin.

Unbleached calico may be had of many widths and textures. Those of the most expensive are usually of the closest and heaviest make; such are not always the best for inner linings, which are required only to give firmness to the vestment, with as little weight as possible. The commoner kinds of this calico are, again, likely to be objectionable, on account of a certain unevenness consequent to their inferior manufacture. It must therefore be left to the judgment of the vestment-maker to choose a medium quality, likely to answer every desirable end. Two errors of a directly opposite character are frequently committed by vestment-makers. The one is the making up of the thinnest and sometimes the poorest fabrics into garments, without an inner lining at all; and the other, the adoption of an inner lining of coarse heavy linen, which weighs down the priest in wearing it, and instead of imparting greater firmness and richness

Church Vestments.

to the robe, gives it a stiff unrelenting appearance, which is unnecessary as it is unseemly.

Vestments of velvet need inner lining even more than those of silk; for velvet is very apt to fall away, through its own weight, from a silk lining only; while it may be held in entire subjection by a closely-tacked layer of unbleached calico.

Unbleached calico possesses one other eminent advantage when compared with whitened calicoes, and even with some linens—lime, or anything else pernicious to gold and evanescent silk dyes, is not used in its fabrication: it is therefore, obviously, the fittest and safest of all accessories, of its kind, to use for vestments with embroideries wrought upon them; which by any evil influence of an evaporative nature, may be damaged as much through the wrong side, as though they were brought into immediate contact with it on the right.

The Importance of Tacking-stitches to the Vestment-maker.

Nothing is more essential to the perfection of vestment-making than a liberal use of tacking-stitches.

Upon a large table, accessible from all sides, the materials to be fashioned should be spread and smoothed out; then first pinned together, here and there, and finally tacked together by stitches never more than an inch long; but they may be less, according to the size of the article being made. Fine reel cotton, *unglazed*, and of *best* quality, should be used for tacking upon rich silken materials and cloth of gold; but fine sewing silk is most proper for tacking upon velvet; as cotton is apt to leave the mark of every stitch, after it is withdrawn, upon the surface of velvet.

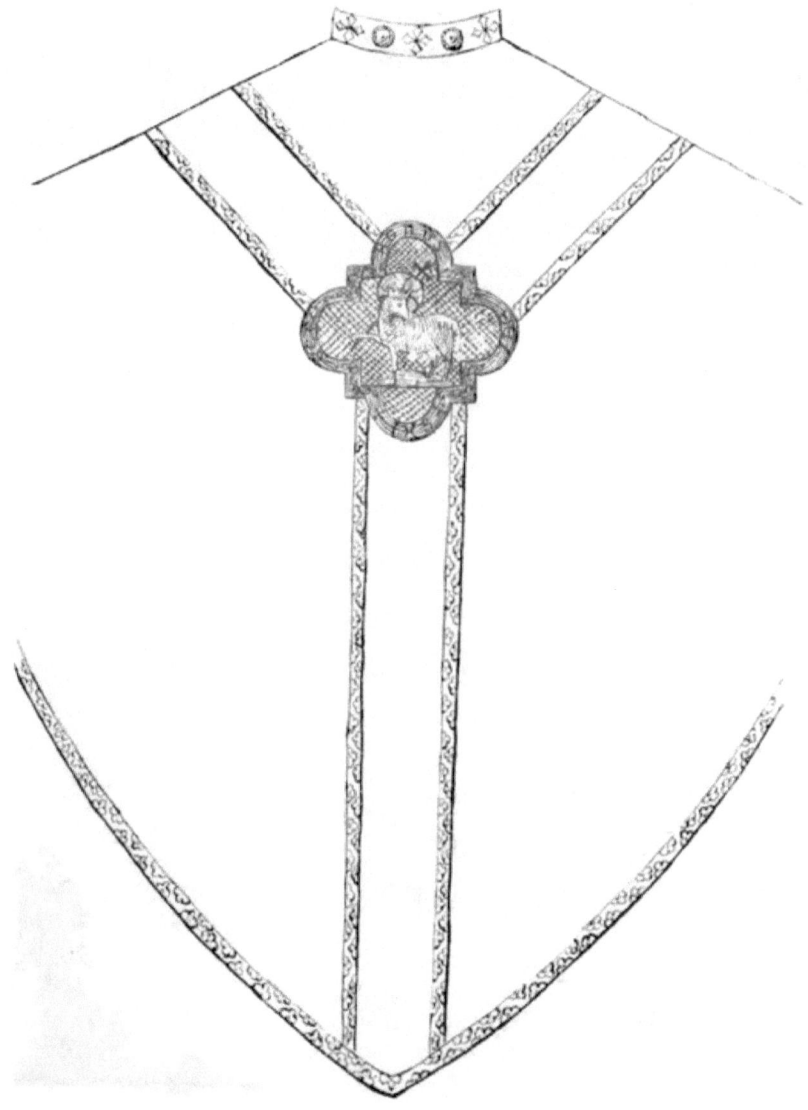

How to make Vestments.

Many persons, who use only the commonest ball cotton for tacking, would accuse us of most wasteful notions in recommending best cotton and sewing silk, for tacking-stitches which are all to be drawn away when the vestment is finished.

As old vestment-makers, we can conscientiously affirm that we never practised the economy, of using common cotton for tacking, without finding it false. Inasmuch, as we have had to endure incalculable chagrin at the disfigurement of lines and holes, upon the surface of costly materials, for every twopenny reel of cotton we have saved.

A needle stouter than necessary for carrying the cotton or silk freely through the work should not be employed for tacking; as it is apt to become a piercer as well as a needle, and, in consequence, to leave a series of small holes permanently made on the surface of the material, after the threads are removed.

Tacking-stitches, whether of silk or cotton, should never be dragged out in long lengths. The thread should be cut here and there at short intervals, and then drawn away.

Church Vestments.

VII.

THE DALMATIC OF THE DEACON.

THE robe worn at High Mass by the deacon is called the *Dalmatic*, a name derived from Dalmatia, from whence this form of garment was first introduced into Rome, where for a long period it was worn only by the emperors, as a vest of distinction.

Pope Sylvester, in the reign of Constantine, first gave to the deacons of the Roman Church the privilege of using the dalmatic at certain solemn services, an honour which, by succeeding pontiffs, was from time to time accorded to the other Churches.

In the most primitive Christian times the robe appointed for the deacon was termed the colobium, literally, the closely-fitting tunic of the better class of citizens in the days of Republican Rome, and which, subsequently, became the dress of the senator. From this point the colobium rose to the dignity of a sacerdotal garment, to be worn by certain ministers at the holy Eucharistic service.

We know that it was thus adopted at a very early period in Christian history, and that a sacred import was attached to it, for as we read, and have elsewhere said, Pope Eutychianus, A.D. 275, forbade the burial of a faithful martyr, unless wrapped in a dalmatic robe, or a purple colobium. The former being, doubtless, held in respect as a covering of the highest worldly distinction; the latter, as the especial garb of the true followers of the

Plate 18.

The Dalmatic.

Saviour, which they put on only in His name, and for the righteous performance of His holy work upon earth, and wearing it, were summoned to their high office about His throne in heaven.

Following closely the description of the colobium as given by correlative authorities, we arrive at the conclusion that, in shape, it was neither more nor less than a very scanty dalmatic, with very short sleeves; in fact, not unlike what the tunic of the subdeacon should be at this day, were the ancient usage strictly adhered to.

In the first days of its use, and for centuries after, the dalmatic was white, ornamented with narrow stripes of scarlet. Fig. 1, Plate 20, is sketched from "The Church of our Fathers;" it is from a fresco painting of the Roman catacombs, so touchingly designated, by the author of the above, as "the metropolis of " Christianity." In this figure we have a clear illustration of the garment decorated with the clavi. Fig. 1, Plate 21, is borrowed from the same book, and presents another instance of the dress of the deacon at a very early period. Here, also, the clavi is distinctly marked. The original copy is described as having been taken "from a very old codex of the Gregorian Sacramentary, belong- " ing, when Martene saw it, to the cathedral library of Autun."

From the sixth century to the present, the dalmatic, as may be seen by the figures on both these Plates, has undergone very slight changes in its shape; and as to the form of its decoration, it can scarcely be said to have altered. For, in the bands of rich lace, or other material, with which the deacon's robe of to-day is ornamented, we have but the ancient Roman clavi more fully represented.

The principal change seems to have been in the substitution of coloured material for the pure white, of which the garment was originally made: this is supposed to have been effected

Church Vestments.

towards the end of the ninth century, and, by the beginning of the twelfth, the dalmatic was more or less adorned with costly materials and needlework, corresponding in splendour, according to the degree of its wearer, with the holy vestment itself.

About this time the wide horizontal apparels on the breast and shoulders of the dalmatic began to appear, and a little later, those similar pieces on the lower part of the vestment were added. These apparels were made the means of embellishing the garment with elaborate needlework, and Dr. Rock tells us that figure subjects were often wrought upon them, "illustrative of "some great event in the annals of our faith." Often, the most memorable passages in the glorious life of that deacon, and first martyr, St. Stephen, and the circumstance of his death especially, were portrayed in these embroideries of the dalmatic.

Sometimes, instead of needlework orphreys, bands of cloth of gold, powdered with pearls, enriched the robe; and, judging from the splendour of every other sacerdotal appointment in the fourteenth century, we may conclude that the deacon's dalmatic lacked no distinguishing ornament at that period.

Amongst the group of ecclesiastics, page 1, taken from the exquisitely limned Psalter of Richard the Second, are a deacon and sub-deacon, correctly robed. In the woodcut, the latter, in his tunicle, is nearest to us; but as his garment only differs from that of the deacon in its length, we are enabled to judge, by comparing this figure, with that of the deacon in our frontispiece, how, exactly, the most approved dalmatic in present use in the Catholic Church, corresponds with that of the fourteenth century.

For many centuries, only the Pope himself could wear the dalmatic beneath the chasuble; then, as a great privilege, certain prelates were permitted to do so; and finally, the favour was

Plate 19

The Dalmatic.

conceded to all bishops, for the celebration of High Mass. As see frontispiece. This custom has now endured for ages, and at the present moment, as probably every one knows, the prelate, when arrayed for the grand service of the Eucharist, carries beneath the sacrificial vestment, not only the dalmatic of the deacon, but the tunicle of the sub-deacon as well.

The shape of the dalmatic in France, with its open flapping sleeves, is entirely wrong, and as ungraceful and unauthorized as that of the stinted, scooped-out chasuble we have so emphatically ignored. We need not, therefore, speak further of the French dalmatic.

The due proportions of a correct dalmatic are given on Plate 20. The dimensions are calculated for a priest of average size. In the illustration, the back of the garment is shown: with the exception of the tassels from the shoulders, the front is in every respect the same.

The decoration of the dalmatic is usually confined to the orphreys, which, if not of needlework, may be very properly made of stripes of some richer material than that of the robe itself; or of bands of figured lace, which may be had of beautiful patterns, and suitable widths.

On a plain silk garment, bands of velvet of the same colour, and edged with narrow woven lace, form very seemly orphreys; or, upon a velvet dalmatic there can, in the absence of embroidery, be no more splendid adornment than cloth of gold orphreys, whether figured or plain.

The material of the dalmatic need not necessarily be the same as the chasuble; on the contrary, although it should unmistakably harmonize with that used for the Eucharistic garment, yet it should be held subordinate in every degree to the vestment of the celebrant.

Church Vestments.

For instance, if the cross of the chasuble be richly embroidered, and the ground upon which it is laid be powdered with holy symbols and figures, the dalmatic may also have things of sacred signification figured upon it;—or it may be of plain silk, such as that of the vestment before it was sprinkled, and the stripes, which should embrace the general effect of colour displayed in the work upon the chasuble, may be actually, and with strict propriety, less rich than the orphreys of the latter.

The vertical bands of the dalmatic, if of lace, should never be less than two and a half inches wide; and if formed of velvet, or other rich plain material, they should not exceed four and a half inches, including a half-inch lace as a bordering on each side.

The horizontal orphreys may be made of lace of six inches wide and ten inches long, or their width in velvet, etc., may be six and a half inches, inclusive of the half-inch lace binding.

To make up the dalmatic the same principles are to be followed as urged for the chasuble. An inner lining of unbleached calico should in most cases be used, and the garment always bordered round with an inch lace, or fringe, or with both, as shown on the frontispiece. Where lace is employed, fringe may be dispensed with; but there can be no question as to its enhancement of the richness of the robe.

The Tunic.

VIII.

THE TUNIC, OR TUNICLE, OF THE SUB-DEACON.

IT might seem almost unnecessary to say anything expressly in regard to this robe, since it is now, with rare exceptions, made in every respect the same as the dalmatic.

But, as it did not always bear this exact resemblance to the deacon's vestment, we are bound to remark upon it.

Like every other article of dress originally adapted to the sacred functions of the priesthood, the sub-deacon's vestment was symbolic, signifying in its curtailed dimensions, as compared with those of the dalmatic, that the wearer, for the time being, was of inferior rank to the deacon. It was shorter in the skirt, and less wide and long in the sleeves than the robe of the latter, and at first was a perfectly plain garment, without stripe or decoration whatever upon it, as may be seen on Plate 21, fig. 2.

In the sixth century, the sub-deacons of the Church wore, instead of a tunic, a pure white alb, when assisting at the holy service; as, in fact, in more primitive times, did all the ministers of the altar, from the bishop downwards.

We find, that it was not until the dawn of the fourteenth century that the name of *tunicle* was bestowed on this robe of the Church. Previously, it had in some places been called the "subtile;" and, by the Anglo-Saxons, "roc," meaning a coat; but, however it may have been named, it had been in use before the sixth century, when St. Gregory the Great lived, for he is

Church Vestments.

mentioned as having deprived sub-deacons of the privilege of wearing it, ordering them, instead, to assume the alb, as worn in far-off times.

Succeeding pontiffs allowed the use of the tunicle to be resumed, and so for ages, up to the present, it has been recognised as the correct liturgical robe of the sub-deacon, who at the celebration of the Mass stands lowest in order of the three officiating ministers.

Formerly, the dalmatic and tunicle of the bishop, who, as we have already said, wears both these garments under his chasuble when he pontificates, were of a heavenly blue,* and of the richest material, exquisitely ornamented with gold embroidery, in luxuriant patterns extending over the breast, back, and shoulders; as, also, around the sleeves and edges of the garments.

During the twelfth century, permission was given to ecclesiastical assistants of lower degree than sub-deacons to wear the tunicle. On great solemnities, cross-bearers, thurifers, taper-bearers, and holy-water carriers, were arrayed in tunicles.

The custom is still followed in many Roman Catholic churches, more particularly as regards the cross-bearer, whom we constantly see at a grand service, heading a procession, beautifully vested after this manner.

Although the dimensions of the tunicle may continue, as they have now almost universally become, identical with those of the dalmatic, yet we fain would see some of the distinction of olden times kept between them in the way of ornament. For, as to the length and width of either garment, as it is worn indiscriminately by different priests of various heights and proportions, a

---

* This colour was to symbolize the Aaronic vesture, commenting upon which our authority says:—"Whether the ornaments as well as the colour peculiar to the Aaronic vesture were "adopted by the Anglo-Saxons, and a row of tiny bells hung around the hem of the bishop's "purple tunicle in this country, as we know was done abroad, cannot now be ascertained."

Plate 2

Fig 1　　　　Fig 2

DEACON AND SUB-DEACON FROM VERY ANCIENT EXAMPLES

The Tunic.

dalmatic of an average size on a tall deacon may scarcely reach his knees; he will then look like a sub-deacon; while, clothed after the same manner, a sub-deacon of diminutive size may be made to appear as though he had assumed the deacon's vestment.

It is certain, then, that if an evident mark of distinction be considered essential, on either of these robes, to the due observance of liturgical rectitude, it can only be shown in the decoration. Acting upon this principle, we have frequently made the tunic with the vertical stripes behind and before, but without the wide horizontal bands, which should always characterize the dalmatic.

IX.

THE SACRIFICIAL STOLE.

THE first name by which this article of sacerdotal dress was called, and by which only it was known for centuries, was " orarium;" by some supposed to have been derived from *ora*, face; and by others from *orare*, to pray. Either, or both of these conclusions are worthy of acceptation, as the origin of the *orarium* was a long strip of linen, not unlike the sacramental humeral veil which the early Christian worshippers wore around their necks, to be used, at one time, as a handkerchief for wiping and covering the face, and at another, during intervals of prayer, to be spread over the shoulders and about the figure.

In many of the paintings of the Roman catacombs the orarium is seen on the female figure, drawn over the head, and partly shrouding the same, after the manner in which some of the old masters loved to drape the head of the blessed Virgin. Fig. 1, Plate 22, is taken from " Hierurgia," where it is titled thus: " A " female at prayer, veiled with the *stole* or *orarium*. This figure " is painted on the walls of the fourth chamber in the cemetery " of Callistus on the Appian Way." The veiling of the female head at time of prayer was, no doubt, as the author of the above asserts, in obedience to the injunction of St. Paul, concerning the devout comportment of women in the presence of God, in His Church (1 Cor. xi. 5).

It was about the eighth century when the old Latin name

The Sacrificial Stole.

orarium was exchanged for the Greek word *stole*, signifying a cloak or mantle of any description to be worn by either sex, but especially by women. Like every other distinguishing article of apparel in the early days of Christian rites, the orarium had its ornamental stripes and fringes of purple, which were carried around its edges.

Then, embroidery was bestowed upon it, at first of a simple character, but afterwards of so elaborate and costly a kind as to render the *orarium* unfit for its primitive purpose as a handkerchief; notwithstanding, it continued to be worn as a part of the honourable insignia of the priestly office, and the *maniple* was now first adopted to answer the useful requirements of the minister.

Subsequently, the *maniple* was, in its turn, deprived by embellishment of its practical qualities; but upon this we have to speak at large, under its own head.

With the increasing ornamentation of the stole, its width gradually contracted, although it diminished not in length, until nearly every portion of the plain material was cut away from the centre, to leave little else but the richly-worked borders, which originally outlined the wide *orarium* of linen.

The stole must have been of narrow dimensions at a very early period, as those figures from mosaics of the sixth century on Plate 5 will show. And we can clearly judge how very little it must have varied after its uttermost reduction in width, by comparing the examples on Plate 6, and those of the thirteenth century on Plate 9, with those figures above named.

It would seem almost incredible, had we not so many edifying proofs that it is a fact, that for twelve hundred years this symbol, or badge, of the Christian priesthood could have been maintained of nearly an undeviating form.

In its first stage the narrow stole was of one width from end

Church Vestments.

to end, as the wider orarium had been; then it appears to have slightly expanded at the ends, and thus throughout the Western Church it has remained up to the present time; for what is called the Gothic stole in these days is simply a fac-simile of the stole on those figures of the twelfth and thirteenth centuries, Plate 9.

But there is a stole of a shape upon which we must remark, with which we meet on many monumental effigies and brasses, more particularly during the fourteenth century. It is a perfectly straight, narrow stole, with an oblong square at the ends, like the top of the *Tau* cross. Such a stole is figured upon the brass of Esmond de Burnedish, in Brundish Church, Suffolk, A.D. 1360; also, on that of Peter de Lacy, in Northfleet Church, Kent, A.D. 1375.

The Council of Laodicæa, A.D. 364, forbade the use of the stole to lectors and sub-deacons, appointing only priests and deacons to wear it. Before the dalmatic came to be generally worn by the deacon, the liturgical dress of this minister was an alb, often richly worked, of ample dimensions, with a stole, the distinguishing emblem of his order, hanging from the left shoulder, as see Plate 22, where a bishop is represented in the act of blessing, attended by a deacon. These figures were taken for "Hierurgia" from an ancient pontifical of the ninth century. In reference to this Dr. Rock observes:—"This ancient rite is "noticed, and the reason for it is assigned by the fourth Council "of Toledo (A.D. 633) : 'Unum igitur orarium oportet Levitam "gestare in sinistro humero, propter quod orat, id est, "praedicat.'"

By the beginning of the tenth century, all deacons throughout the Christian world officiated at the grand celebration of the Mass, clothed in the dalmatic, with the stole beneath it, still worn

Plate 22
THE ORARIUM

THE DEACON'S STOLE

The Sacrificial Stole.

over the left shoulder, but crossed over the body, behind and before, to be attached under the right arm. In this manner does the deacon continue to wear the stole; while the celebrant, who until the end of the fourteenth century let his stole hang straight down as bishops and some members of religious orders do now, crosses it over his breast, as it was placed at his ordination, and embraces it by the girdle of his alb.

The stole was no longer made of linen after its use was exclusively confined to the priests officiating at the Eucharistic service, but was formed, as now, of materials to correspond with the sacrificial vestments with which it was worn.

In the Eastern Churches, the stole is as important a part of the sacerdotal vestiary as it is with us. The stole of the Greek priest is worn around the neck; that of the deacon rests over the left shoulder, to hang straight down, until the Communion, when it is crossed over the breast, and its ends made to encircle the waist.

The ornamentation of the stole of the Greek deacon is fully indicative of the solemnity attached to this portion of the liturgical dress by the Greek Church; it consists of the word "Holy," inscribed in three different places upon it.

The sacrificial stole of priest and deacon, made after the approved Gothic model, is 3 yards long,* and, measuring from the half *downwards*—whereby a length of one yard and a half, or 54 inches, is described—it is regulated in *width* as follows:—

At the centre, behind, it is $2\frac{3}{4}$ inches wide.
At the end of 10 inches, it is 3 inches wide.
At the end of 34 inches, it is $3\frac{1}{4}$ inches wide.
At the end of 44 inches, it is $3\frac{1}{2}$ inches wide.

* The stole generally worn when St. Osmund's Use was framed was full 10 feet long, and little more than 2 inches wide.

Church Vestments.

And, for the remaining 10 inches, continues to expand from 3½ inches, till it reaches a width of 6 inches at the extreme end.

We may seem to be unduly precise in these directions for the shape of the stole; but, as its symmetry depends so much upon its almost imperceptible increase in width, we cannot believe that we have wasted a word in explaining the manner of accomplishing this nicety of gradation.

There are numerous ways of ornamenting the sacrificial stole; but whatever else may be the design worked upon it, a cross at each end, and one in the middle of the back, are strictly required by the Church.

These crosses may be either simple or florid, wrought only in gold—for gold is allowed by the Rubric to represent every colour but black and purple—or with colours reflected from the needlework of the vestment, mingled with gold.

On Plate 34 we offer patterns or, more properly, suggestions for the decoration of the stole, which, by the way, should always correspond as nearly as possible with the ornamentation on the other vestments.

The materials of which the sacrificial stole is made should be the same as those of the vestment with which it is to be used. From one yard and a half of silk, of 24 inches wide, the stoles of the celebrant and the deacon may be cut, as it is quite admissible, and usual, to join the stole exactly in the centre of the back, and to embroider or to transfer the cross over the seam.

The quantity of silk named is calculated for stoles which are to be bound, as we have described for the chasuble, with lace, and will not therefore require turnings to be left in the superior material.

But if it be planned to have a cord edging, the upper silk must be as wide as the lining, that each may turn inwards to

The Sacrificial Stole.

make a neat edge for the cord to be sewn along. It is clear then that a 24-inch silk, or fabric of any kind, will not cut two stoles of the regulation width, if turnings be required.

This being beyond our control, we can only give hints on the subject, which may be sometimes acted upon with advantage.

The making up of the stole depends in a great measure upon its needlework adornment. If only the three crosses be worked upon it, a half-inch border of woven lace will add materially to its comeliness; and if it be handsomely embroidered the whole way along, as it frequently is, a simple cord sewn along its edges will be in the best taste.

The fringe—for the stole should always be fringed at its ends*— may be from 2 to 3 inches deep. One deeper than this is not advisable, as it is apt to catch awkwardly, and arrest the solemn movements of the minister, or to get generally disordered and unseemly looking in a short space of time.

Where gold has been used in the embellishment of the stole, there is an excuse for a plain gold fringe, which is always a suitable appendage; or, the colours in the needlework may be mixed through the fringe and streaked, as it were, with gold. According to our theory, as set forth in "Church Embroidery," page 167, the last named would be the most correct fringe for a stole with variegated embroidery enriched by gold, as it would appear to be, what a fringe originally was—the very fabric itself frayed out.

Where the three crosses are to be the only adornment of the

---

* In ancient times the stole had a row of little silver or gold bells fastened along its ends. These appendages, which were called "tintinnabulum," and, sometimes, "campanula," denoted great honour and dignity.

In lieu of these little bells, twisted chains of silver and gold, of exquisite workmanship, with glittering pendants of the same precious metals, were often attached to the old English stole.

Church Vestments.

stole, there is a much-adopted plan of working them, for transfer, on velvet pasted upon holland, cutting them out afterwards, and leaving a mere suspicion of velvet beyond the edging cord. This expedient answers well, particularly for a simple cross, with a bold outline, and is commendable for two principal reasons. The first being, that the rich material of the stole is saved from risk of damage, should it not be convenient to finish the embroidery off at once; and, the second, that it enables the worker to dispense with a large frame; as a frame of 18 inches long will answer as well for the process of transferring as for the embroidery.

The Roman stole is wider and shorter than that of the old Gothic type, and joined in the centre by a seam cut on the cross, as see Plate 34, that it may set smoothly round the neck. Its usual dimensions are 8 feet 6 inches long by $4\frac{1}{2}$ inches broad, till within 6 inches of the end, where it begins to expand to a width of $9\frac{1}{2}$ inches at the extreme end. Owing to the extended width of the Roman stole, larger crosses are, very consistently, usually employed for its embellishment than can be figured upon the Gothic stole.

X

THE MANIPLE.

THE Maniple was first brought into use to take the place of the stole, the primitive object of which, as a handkerchief, had been defeated by the elaborate ornamentation expended upon it by the zealous supporters of the rites of the Church, who seemed unable to endure the existence of any article appertaining to the functions of the ministers at the holy altar, that was not as rich in fabrication as human means could make it.

Originally the maniple was a strip of linen, as the stole had been, but narrower and shorter, and suspended, as it now is, from the left arm. In the same manner must table attendants have carried the napkin in olden times, as instanced from Strutt, on Plate 33. The figure is taken from a group representing Lot entertaining the two angels.

At first, from its use as a handkerchief to wipe the perspiration from the face and brow of the minister, the sacerdotal maniple was called "Sudarium." In the "Golden Legend" it is said of Peter "that he bare alway a '*sudary*,' to wipe the teerys y' ranne "from his eyen."

After the maniple had, in course of time, become too ornamental for the fulfilment of its first design, it was retained as a symbol of the sacred calling of the ministry; and finally, towards the eighth century, it began to be made of the same material as the sacrificial vestments, and was numbered among them.

Church Vestments.

Even in the sixth century we find that St. Gregory the Great was solicited by John, Archbishop of Ravenna, in behalf of his minor clergy, for permission to wear, as the clergy then did at Rome, the maniple while waiting on the Archbishop. His Holiness granted the favour, but it was not to be extended beyond the first deacons of the Church at Ravenna.

By the ninth century, deacons as well as priests had assumed the maniple, but it was nigh upon the twelfth century before sub-deacons received it at their ordination, and were appointed to use it ever afterwards, as an honourable badge of their ministerial office, at the solemn service of the High Mass.*

Three maniples, to be worn by the celebrant, deacon, and sub-deacon, must always be made to complete a full set of vestments. They should be decorated and formed like the stoles in every way but in length; they must measure only 44 inches from end to end.

The Pugin maniple is but 40 inches, and is adopted by many priests in preference to that of longer dimensions.

The latter is considered to be the most correct by others, who only favour the oldest examples.

After the maniple is made, it should be folded in half, and caught together and sewn by the lining, straight across, at a distance of 6 inches from the centre, to form a loop for the arm of the priest to pass through. A tab of silk, like the lining, measuring one by three-quarters of an inch, must also be sewn inside near the edge, and on a line with the centre cross, that the maniple may be pinned to the sleeve of the alb, on the upper side of the arm.

* In the Oriental Churches, in lieu of the maniple, a crimson apparel, which encircles the arm for some inches, like a cuff, is worn upon each wrist. These apparels are usually decorated with gold embroidery; but sometimes, in the Greek Church, they are figured with the bust of our Lord, which is presented to be kissed by the faithful, who approach the prelate.

The Maniple.

A clerk who is not yet in holy orders may sometimes be called upon to fill the office of sub-deacon; in such case, it will be understood that he is not entitled to wear the maniple, as the privilege can only be enjoyed by those who have been duly ordained as priests.

The maniple is the first thing put on by the priest robing for the Mass, upon the removal of his cope, after the return, of the procession of the Asperges, to the Sanctuary.

The Roman maniple is 36 inches long, the same width as, and ornamented to correspond with, the stole.

XI.

THE STOLONE.

THE Stolone is the wide stole for which the deacon exchanges his folded chasuble during the celebration of the Grand Mass, on most days throughout Lent and Advent, and upon solemn feasts, such as that of the Purification.

The stolone is of black on Good Friday, and of purple at other times; in short, of the same colour and material as the vestments of the day.

Crosses at the ends, and at the back, generally constitute its needlework ornamentation. It is usually bordered with a figured silk lace, and fringed, to correspond with the other sacrificial garments.

The stolone should be 9 feet long and 10 inches wide, and as it is worn like the ordinary stole of the deacon, *i. e.*, over the left shoulder and attached under the right arm, it should be caught together by the two edges, at a distance of 27 inches down, measuring from the cross in the middle of the back.

The deacon exchanges his chasuble for the stolone before the Gospel, and does not resume the former garment till after the Elevation, and before the Post-Communion is read.

The Confessional Stole.

XII.

THE CONFESSIONAL STOLE.

THE Confessional Stole is always of violet, the penitential colour, figured with simple crosses of gold, or of gold colour.

It is usually about 2½ inches, or seldom more than 3 inches wide, and, more often than not, is of the same width from end to end, and 2¾ yards long.

It may be lined, either with violet, or with gold colour; the former is generally preferred.

Church Vestments.

XIII.

THE BAPTISMAL STOLE.

TWO Stoles, one of purple, the other of white, are required for the Baptismal Service.

The purple stole is put on by the priest at the beginning of the ceremony, and worn until the words "Dost thou believe," etc., are about to be pronounced, when it is exchanged for the white stole.

Although sometimes a stole, purple on one side and white upon the other, is made to answer the purpose of the two distinct stoles, yet it is a custom only tolerated by the Church where sheer necessity, arising from lack of means, can be made the excuse for the expedient.

The violet stole typifies the soul's condition of original sin, before it is received into the Church of Christ. It may be decorated only with simple crosses embroidered in gold, or gold silk, upon the ends and back. On Plate 23 is a florid design for this stole.

The white stole is assumed as a symbol of the purification of the soul by the holy rite of Baptism. It may be of very rich materials and work.

Very elaborate and beautiful designs are frequently worked on the white baptismal stole, particularly, as is not unusual, when the parents, or the sponsors of the infant, present the priest with the stoles for the ceremony.

DESIGNS FOR STOLES

The Baptismal Stole.

The baptismal stole is worn pendent, *i.e.*, not crossed upon the breast, and is best made a full half-yard shorter than the stole for the Holy Mass.

It may also be wider than the last-mentioned, and if more than 3 inches wide in the middle, may be joined slantwise like the Roman stole, in order that it may fit well round the neck.

Only gold, silver, or gold colour, may be used on the white baptismal stole. *Silver* embroidery on the white ground is very chaste and lovely, and may be used to any extent. There is but one objection to it—its aptitude to tarnish quickly.

A suitable pattern for the white baptismal stole is given on Plate 23. It should be lined, and finished off, with fringe at the ends, and with a cord and tassels to confine it over the breast, like the preaching stole.

Church Vestments.

XIV.

THE PREACHING STOLE.

THIS Stole, like the vestments of the altar, must be always of the colour of the day.

It is seldom seen very plainly adorned, having either richly-ornamented crosses worked at the ends, or an embroidered pattern spreading all over it, in addition to the three crosses which must be figured upon every stole.

As the ample and proper surplice is one yard and a quarter long, the preaching stole, which should not fall below the surplice, should be two yards and a quarter long, and somewhat wider than the sacrificial stole. There is no arbitrary rule for the dimensions of the *Gothic* preaching stole; those of the *Roman* standard are as follows:—$2\frac{1}{4}$ yards long, and $4\frac{1}{2}$ inches wide, till within 8 inches of the bottom; it then increases gradually to 9 inches across at the extreme lower end.

As it is joined cross-wise in the middle of the back, that it may set easily round the collar, it is necessary to remark that the measurement of $2\frac{1}{4}$ yards must be secured along the *outer* edge. By the *inner* edge, the length of the Roman preaching stole is 2 yards and 3 inches.

The Gothic as well as the Roman stole should have a handsome fringe along the ends, and a cord and tassels attached to each side, to confine it over the breast of the minister. These appendages may be either of gold, or of a mixture comprising the colours in the work and the shade of the ground, enriched by strands of gold.

Plate 23 exhibits a design for a preaching stole.

XV.

THE COPE.

"THE Cappa (or cope, says Honorius, is the proper robe of singers, cantorum), which seems to be substituted for "the acintine tunic of the law (pro tunicâ acintinâ legis), from "whence, as that was adorned with bells, so this with fringes.*

"By this robe holy conversation is represented, therefore it is "used by every order. It has a hood above, which marks the "joy of Heaven. It reaches to the feet, because in good living "we must persevere to the end; by the fringes the labour is "denoted by which the service of God is consummated. It is "open before, because eternal life lies open to the ministers of "Christ who lead a holy life."

The beautiful symbolism conveyed in the above passage has tempted us to give it as a heading to our chapter on the robe which is thus so piously eulogized.

But, we have to descend to mere matter-of-fact reasoning for the origin of the cope, and are thereby brought to believe that, as its primitive name, pluviale, implies, it was a garment invented to protect the clergy from inclement weather, in out-of-door processions.

The precise period of the adoption of this robe is not known, for early illuminated figures showing its use are rare, and before the time of Edward the Confessor, we gather very little from

---

* The fringe of the Anglo-Saxon cope was frequently formed of little bells of purest gold.

Church Vestments.

he old chronicles, to assist us in fixing the date of its introduction.

In the reign of the king just named, we read of Leofric bequeathing three *copes* for the chanters of his Church of Exeter; and of Queen Matilda, wife of the Conqueror, leaving by her will, to the Abbey of the Trinity, at Caen, of which she was the founder, a richly-worked robe of gold, intended for a *cope*, with two other gorgeous vestments, wrought, as the first named, in England.

Her husband, who so constantly evinced his appreciation of our native talent for sacerdotal adornment, by seizing every beautiful vestment he saw in our churches, to bestow it on his beloved Normandy, sent to St. Hugh, Abbot of Cluny, a most splendid cope, bordered all around the lower edge by a deep fringe of little tinkling bells, of purest gold.

We are also told that at the close of the eleventh century Arnulph, prior of Rochester Monastery, " caused to be made the " principal vestment embroidered with a tree in gold, and the " best cope, and a covering inlaid with precious stones." The chronicler says further, " the cope above mentioned had silver " bells, and that which is there next to it, called ' a covering in- " laid with precious stones,' is an albe with the amice adorned " with precious stones."

Then, of our own Anglo-Saxon Margaret, Queen of Scotland, it is recorded that she caused to be made copes to match in beauty with the numerous other vestments so thoughtfully provided by her, for the service of the Church she so " delighted " to honour."

A record now lies before us of an entry extracted from the Liberate Roll 24, Henry the Third (A.D. 1241), where an item occurs of 24*l*. 1*s*. 6*d*. paid to Adam de Basinges for a red silk

SYMBOLICAL ORPHREY FOR COPE.

The Cope.

cope given by the king to the Bishop of Hereford. This sum, according to the value of money at that time, is computed at upwards of 360*l.* sterling.

It would seem that the vast surface of material presented in the cope was the happy excuse for covering it with the most wonderful things in needlework. Whole histories from Holy Writ, or from the lives of the Saints, have been told over and over again in embroidery, in numberless different ways, on this magnificent robe.* We have already described, as see page 15, some of the most remarkable of the examples left to us of these achievements, and could yet fill a larger volume than we dare allow ourselves to devote, even to the whole of the sacred vestments, in mere descriptions of *copes* alone, that we have seen and read about.

For, of all the garments belonging to the clerical offices of the ancient Christian Church, none are perhaps better known, or have held their original position of dignity under greater favour, through all the various doctrinal changes of the Protestant era, than the cope.

For centuries it has been the robe worn by sovereigns at their coronation, and in it, likewise, does the archbishop and his assistant prelates vest themselves for their part in the same solemn ceremony.

In Durham Cathedral, copes continued to be used up to a period in the last century when the mere mention of amice, alb, or chasuble, would have called forth the indignation, if not the severest admonition, of the whole community of the Established Church.

Of all our grand cathedrals, in old Catholic times, none were

---

* As, for example, those three wonderful copes, of the Monastery of St. Blase in the Black Forest, which are so ably illustrated by Gerbert, in his "Vetus Liturgia Alemannica."

richer in copes than Durham, for every one of its monks could walk in procession clad in a costly cope; while that worn by the prior was of cloth of gold, and so weighted with splendour that, whenever he put it on, those who were his train-bearers, on other occasions, had to support this massive robe on every side.

It was, no doubt, in such churches as this that the custom was followed "of spreading a wide linen cloth in the middle of " the choir floor, and heaping it with a pile of copes to be worn " at the divine service. By this method these garments could be " easily got at just before the clergy had to walk forth in pro- " cession, and as easily put off afterwards."

The cope has always been the processional, as the chasuble the sacrificial, robe of the priest, and is thus set down in the Salisbury Use.

Formerly, "in collegiate and cathedral churches, and wealthier " religious houses, the canons, the monks and friars, and as " many as possible of the elder clergy, were arrayed in silken " copes at the principal services on each Sunday and holiday, " marked for walking in any kind of solemn procession.

"For like reason, the 'rectores chori,' or rulers of the choir, " who on account of their office had to be so often moving to " and fro as they led the singing, not only bore richly-ornamented " staves in their hands, but from the Anglo-Saxon and all through " the English period, were vested too in copes, the most beautiful " which their churches happened to possess."

That which is called the hood of the cope, and which for ages has been nothing else but an ornamental appendage, was originally a real covering for the head, to be worn up or down, at the option of the wearer, according to the weather.

Before the close of the Anglo-Saxon period, the first object of the hood as an appurtenance of utility began to be disregarded,

The Hood of Cope.

and flat pieces of enriched embroidery were often substituted for the former head-covering. It is said, that even sheets of thin solid gold, suspended from the back of the robe by delicate golden hooks and chains, took the place of the hood even before William of Normandy's time. These gorgeous appendages are supposed to have been the "taisselli," of which this king, in his great love for Anglo-Saxon works of value, took iiii from the poor monks of Ely.

After the Normans came, the actual hood of service was entirely abandoned for the flat piece of ornamental needlework which, at this moment, we designate the hood of the cope.

These so-called hoods have always been made to vie with the orphreys in beauty of design and wealth of materials. Upon the hood has generally been figured, by the most skilled hands, subjects of holy events marking the particular high festivals of the Church, and, in mediæval times, some copes had many such hoods, to be used according to the feast in commemoration.

In the old inventories it is singularly interesting to note the descriptions of many of these sacred pictures in *needle-painting:* We have only space to quote a few of the most curious from the Lincoln account:—

"A cope of red cloth of gold, having in the hood the Majesty."

"A red cope of cloth of gold, with costly orphreys, with the "scripture of St. Katherine in the hood, the tomb springing oil;[*] "in the morse, an angel bearing a crown; of the gift of "Mr. John Morton, Archbishop of Canterbury, and Cardinal "of Anastasis."

"A cope of red velvet, broidered with archangels and stars of "gold," and "an image of the crucifix in the hood."

[*] From the tombs of many of the saints a precious kind of oil was said to exude; from that of St. Katherine especially.

Church Vestments.

"Two copes of black satin, orphreys red damask, broidered with flowers of gold, having in the back souls rising to their doom, either of them having in the hood an image of our "Saviour sitting upon the rainbow."

The salutation of our Lady, the Assumption, and the Coronation of the Virgin, frequently form the subjects on the hoods in these lists.

The lovely Syon cope is unfortunately without a hood now, but the golden loops which suspended it below the orphrey still remain, to keep us for ever speculating and wondering as to the treasure we have lost. For, the hood of that cope could have been naught but an object for lovers of the ancient faith to glory in.

The hood of the Anglo-Saxon priest was, at first, of a pointed triangular shape; but, in course of time, its outline took a more curved and relenting form, in obedience to the principles of the advancing taste in sacred art, and finally settled into the symmetrical figure of an inverted Gothic arch. This was the shape of the hood of the cope in the middle of the sixteenth century, and the same which, at this day, is the only one acknowledged to be correct by the best authorities on sacred vesture. The semi-circular hood is a comparatively modern invention, inelegant, and inconsistent with ancient associations of the Church. The hood, to be proper, should not exceed 18 inches across the top; the depth of the same to the extreme point should scarcely measure more than 21 inches. The designs on Plate 25 are for hoods 15 inches wide by 18 inches deep.

The orphreys of the cope, as of old, should match with the hood in wealth and beauty. They may be made of any width from 5 to 10 inches: less than the one makes a poor and insignificant orphrey; more than the latter is apt to produce a coarse, rather than a rich, effect.

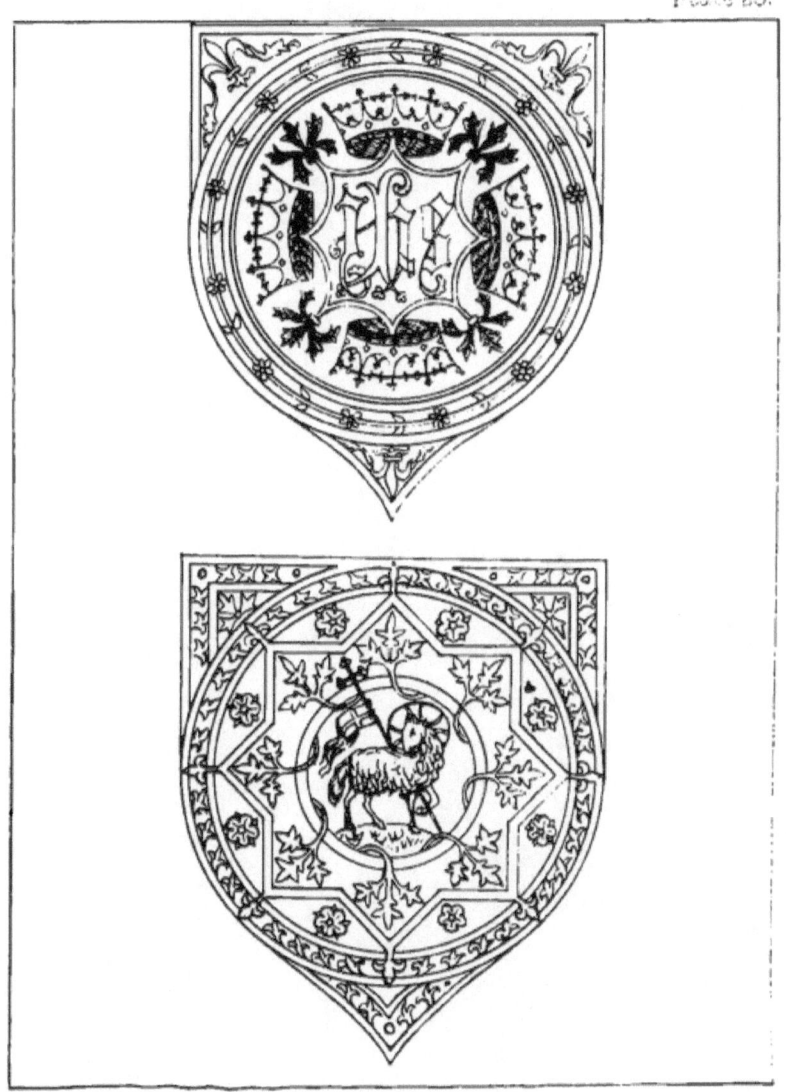

HOODS FOR COPES

Orphreys of Cope.

An eight-inch orphrey was the most favoured in ancient times, and it is very seemly, and affords ample space for a handsome pattern of either canopied saints, flowers, scroll-work, or geometrical figures.

Formerly, these orphreys must have been more splendid with the embroidery, gold, pearls, precious stones, and enamels heaped upon them, than the warmest enthusiast in these utilitarian days can conceive. We must remember, too, that the material of the robe itself was very frequently like the Syon cope, and others we know about, worked all over in the richest and most elaborate manner with wonderful designs of saints, and angels, and holy symbols of every kind. Animals, and birds of conventional forms and spiritualized expression, were also often introduced in these vast diapered patterns of the cope, and contributed, apart from the precious metals and stuffs wrought about them, no small degree of grandeur and mystery of effect to the more exalted emblems of religion.

Sometimes, as now, these patterns would be figured in the loom, on grounds of gold, rich velvet, or silk, and not by the embroideress. But, in such case, the orphreys of the garment, and the hood, would be, generally, of elaborate needlework.

A cope of this kind is shown on our Frontispiece. The main portion of the robe is supposed to be of a woven material; the hood, and the orphreys, of embroidery.

The following are the correct dimensions for a cope of the true shape; by which we mean that of a *cycloid*, instead of an *exact semicircle*, of which this robe is generally supposed to be formed. If cut upon the latter principle, the cope loses much of the grace and dignity of its ancient prototype. For, supposing the garment to be made from a circle of 10 feet across, it must

Church Vestments.

necessarily be 5 feet long behind; and, when laid over the shoulders, and duly taken up by their breadth, it is obvious that it will have the appearance of being much shorter before than it is behind: unless it be made from a circle of larger dimensions, when the cope, in order that it may in a seemly manner cover the feet in front, will rest upon the ground several inches at the back.

To counteract these objections, the curve must be drawn out from the generating point upon the circle to the *common cycloid* form; so that, in fact, if the right length of the cope behind be 5 feet, it may measure along its straight edge 11 feet. The cope in the Frontispiece is sketched from a model of these dimensions. The cope, with the exception of the humeral veil, is the least difficult of all the sacred garments to make up, always providing that it be laid out on a large table, closely *tacked*, and otherwise proceeded with, as recommended, page 73.

An inner lining of stout unbleached calico is required for it; some vestment-makers use coarse linen, which many priests object to, on account of its weight, *without value*. As for every other vestment, this inner lining must be cut to the exact shape which the garment is to be when made, and the rich material tacked upon it. Then, the silk lining is to be placed and the three-quarters of an inch, left beyond the size, turned over upon the superior material, to be covered by the orphrey at the upper, and by the narrow border of needlework, lace binding, or fringe, at the lower, edge. A fringe round the bottom of the cope is not greatly approved by the clergy at the present day; they say it is apt to catch, and occasion awkward movements, especially as regards the processional garment. Notwithstanding this objection, a fringe is the most graceful of all appendages for the robe, and as such was the most favoured in past days; when, as

Colour of Cope.

we have already said, it was frequently made even of tiny bells of the precious metals.

The cope must always be of the colour of the day, and when worn with the sacrificial vestments, should correspond with them, not only in colour, but in ornamentation.

A cope of the colour of the day is assumed by the priest who is honoured, as the assistant of the bishop, at a Pontifical High Mass. *Vide* Frontispiece.

When the divine service is not celebrated by a prelate, the ordinary officiant wears the cope only in the procession of the asperges from the sacristy to the altar, and from thence through the church. Upon the return to the sanctuary the cope is removed from the shoulders of the priest, and he assumes the sacrificial robe—the chasuble, to remain thus clothed to the end of the solemn service.

At the benediction of the blessed Sacrament the priest wears a white cope.

The same in the procession on Holy Thursday.

On the Feast of the Purification, the processional cope is purple.

For the divine office before and after the midnight Mass at Christmas, either a white, or a gold cope, is put on by the officiant at the ninth lesson. At the same time, the cantors array themselves in white copes.

On Holy Saturday a purple cope is used by the celebrant, and, should a bishop officiate, he wears a purple cope at the blessing of the fire, and also at the benediction of the font.

On the Vigil of Pentecost a purple cope is worn at the benediction of the font.

On the Feast of Corpus Christi, white processional copes are used.

Church Vestments.

During the office of the First Vespers for the Commemoration of the Dead, which immediately follows the Second Vespers of the Feast of All Saints, the priest is clothed in a black cope.

Also, in Masses for the Dead, where a cope is used, it must be black; upon which white, only, may be figured.

The Morse.

The morse is the ornamental fastening by which the cope is confined upon the breast of the wearer. In the oldest of our Church inventories we find profuse mention of the morse, and may be justified in dating its adoption from a period almost as early as that of the cope itself.

In the list of vestments of old St. Paul's, made A.D. 1295, twenty-eight morses are enumerated as of superlative value, most of them being of goldsmiths' work, and embellished with jewels and enamels. A morse of this costly kind is illustrated in the translation of M. Jules Labarte's work on the "Arts of the "Middle Ages and Renaissance." It is described as follows:—
"Silver gilt. Fourteenth century. Forms a quatrefoil, with small "lobes at the points of intersection. A lozenge, edged with "cabochons of various colours and pearls, is inscribed within the "quatrefoil, and on it is an eagle crowned; the wings and body "enriched with precious stones, rubies, sapphires, and garnet "cabochons. Diameter, 7 inches."*

No doubt, anciently the art of the lapidary and the worker in precious metals was extensively encouraged, and exercised in the production of the morse, as many of those beautiful examples of the sacred jewel existing in different collections of ancient

---

* Descriptions of many such as this are to be found in the Inventories of Lincoln, York Minster, St. George's Collegiate Chapel, Windsor; and of many others taken before, and during the sixteenth century.

The Morse.

treasures abroad, as well as at home, will show. So, likewise, must the skill of the needleworker have been equally in request, as evidenced in nearly every familiar chronicle of Church vesture. Some of these embroidered morses are described, as belonging to those gorgeous red velvet copes of Lincoln, on page 14.

It was not unusual to embroider the name of the donor of the robe, in the form of a rebus or otherwise, on the morse, accompanied by some pious inscription, such as a supplication for prayers for his soul, as instanced in the gift of Robert Thornton, page 20. The coat of arms of the benefactor of the cope was also a favourite secular device for the morse. We read of the arms of Lord William Smith, Bishop of Lincoln, A.D. 1495, being wrought on the morses of no fewer than twenty-five splendid copes in succession.

Subjects from Holy Writ, in affinity with the history delineated on the garment itself, were frequently figured upon the morse in the middle ages; and very elaborately must they have been worked, to render them intelligible on the necessarily small space to which the design was limited.

Gold and gems, too, were profusely used about these embroideries, until they were sometimes made to be even more costly, as they were often more precious, owing to the devout hands that worked them, than the massive clasp of the skilled goldsmith.

The morse of pure gold or silver, studded with precious jewels, is not in these modern times so liberally bestowed upon the cope as formerly. A fastening fashioned in needlework is now, more often than any other, seen upon the garment; and is certainly preferable, for its genuineness alone, to any clasp of spurious metals and unreal stones. Six inches by five is a favoured size for an embroidered morse. For its ornamentation, either of the following is a suitable design :—

Church Vestments.

A good geometrical figure, consistent with the pattern upon the cope or its orphreys; the cross of England's patron saint, St. George, upon a shield; the monogram, or the emblems of the saint or martyr to whom the church for which the cope is made is dedicated; or, better than all, the monogram of our Lord, or a figure of His Cross; for, no matter what the cope may be, these holy symbols can be shown in no more fitting place than on the breast of His ministers.

The Offertory Veil.

XVI.

THE OFFERTORY VEIL.

THIS vestment is sometimes called the *Humeral Veil*, and again, the *Benediction Veil*. Although neither of these terms may be considered incorrect, yet the Offertory Veil seems to be the most appropriate, insomuch as it bears an immediate reference to the especially solemn part of the Divine service, during which the sub-deacon wears the garment.

As the celebrant is repeating the Offertorium, the sub-deacon advances from the foot of the altar to the credence table, where the chalice and paten, prepared for the sacrifice, are placed, covered by the offertory veil. Assisted by an acolyte, he arranges this veil over his shoulders, and, tying it in front, envelops the sacred vessels by it, and proceeds with them, thus shrouded, to the epistle side of the altar, where the deacon receives them from him.

After the offering of the chalice and paten, the deacon returns the latter to the sub-deacon, who, taking it in hands already muffled in the veil, retires to the foot of the altar, where he continues to hold the sacred vessel, in the attitude shown in the Frontispiece, till the end of the Pater Noster.

This function of the sub-deacon " is said to date from the " time when the faithful offered bread and wine on the paten. " As these offerings were large, the size of the paten was in " proportion, and, being inconvenient on the altar, it was

Church Vestments.

"removed, and held by the sub-deacon till wanted again by "the priest."*

Dr. Rock says that "in old Catholic England an acolyte, clad "in an alb and tunicle, and not the sub-deacon, so held the "paten at High Mass." By some of the ancient writers the acolyte thus appointed was called the "patener."

The use of the offertory veil is supposed to have existed from a very early period in Anglo-Saxon times, although its history is somewhat vague up to the eleventh century, when we find Leofric, Bishop of Exeter, bequeathing to his church "iiii sub-"diaconis handlin," which, it is concluded, were offertory veils.

This vestment is always of the colour of the day, and made to harmonize in every other respect with the sacrificial robes with which it is worn.

It is fashioned as a straight scarf, measuring full 3 yards long, and varying from 20 to 36 inches in width. The veil shown in the Frontispiece is a medium width of 27 inches, and is that which is generally approved. A narrow offertory veil of 18, or even 20 inches wide, unless it be made of a very rich material, is a spare-looking and undignified garment; notwithstanding, it is by no means uncommon to see such an one in use, particularly when it accompanies a suit of vestments of either the Italian or French form.

A rich piece of embroidery, symbolical of the elements of the blessed Sacrament; or a design of the Lamb of the Holy Sacrifice; or the letters of the name of our Lord, surrounded by rays of glory, are alike proper for the ornamentation of the offertory veil. Sometimes, added to an elaborate piece of needlework in the centre, an embroidered border, such as we have practically illustrated towards the end of this volume, is carried

---

* Rev. F. Oakeley, M.A. : "Order and Ceremonial of the Mass."

CENTRES FOR CROSS ON CHASUBLE.

The Offertory Veil.

all about the edges of this scarf. Otherwise, a suitable woven lace is used to bind it round, after the manner already described for other vestments. It should always be finished along the ends by a fringe of at least 3 inches deep.

Ribbon strings of 2 inches wide, and half a yard long, or silk cords, terminating in tassels, should be sewn at each side on the front edge of the veil, that the minister may tie it across his breast.

These strings are ordinarily sewn at a distance of a yard apart—measuring from the centre of the veil, 18 inches each way.

The lining of the offertory veil should be of silk, the same as that used for the other vestments of the day. The employment of a woollen material for this purpose is not only incorrect, but reprehensible. Where paucity of means forbids silk, pure fine linen may be substituted with impunity. Such a lining, when soiled, may be easily taken out and washed; and, further, linen, of all fabrics, has the highest sanction for proximity to the sacred vessels.

Church Vestments.

XVII.

THE CHALICE VEIL.

THE Chalice Veil, used in the Western Church, is the small square of silk, like the vestments of the day, which overspreads the chalice and paten, as they are being conveyed to and from the sacristy, and which covers them while resting on the credence table.

The size of this veil may vary from a square of 24, to one of 20 inches. It is usually distinguished by a cross of needlework, which may be either ornamental, or plain. To place the cross, as shown on Plate 28, the silk should be folded in three one way, and precisely in half the other; and where the lines meet on the first creased* division of the silk, *there* should the centre of the cross be fixed. By this arrangement the cross falls naturally in front, when the veil is laid evenly over the sacred vessels.

It is not incorrect to work the cross precisely in the centre of the chalice veil; indeed, it is the Italian custom so to do, although the practice of placing the ornament in front is the most favoured by the English clergy.

The chalice veil may have an embroidered border, like the offertory veil, as well as the cross, and may be still further enriched by a fringe of 2½ inches deep.

* It will be unnecessary to make any more permanent mark than a crease for this indication.

The Chalice Veil.

Ordinarily, it has a woven lace of an inch wide, to match with that of the vestments, laid flat round its edges: the addition of a fringe is optional.

No other but a silk, or a fine linen lining, must be thought of for this veil. Failing the former material, the latter, as in the case of the offertory veil, to be the sole substitute.

Church Vestments.

XVIII.

THE BURSE.

THE Burse is the familiar name for the corporal case, the square, firm kind of pocket, which always accompanies the sacred vessels at the Holy Mass.

It should be made of the same materials as the sacrificial vestments, and as it is the receptacle for the corporal,* the cloth upon which the sacred elements are consecrated, it must never be lined with anything but the finest white lawn.

The size of the burse varies from 9 to 12 inches square. It has usually a cross worked upon it, of a design and treatment assimilating with the ornament displayed on the vestments of the day. Sometimes a border of needlework, as described for the chalice veil, instead of the more common border of woven lace, is made to encompass the cross; or a conventional pattern is elegantly arranged to overspread the entire surface of the case, as see Plate 28.

Anciently, it was the custom to embellish the burse in the richest manner, and to elaborate beautifully, even on the small space the article afforded for the due development of figures, subjects from the lives of our Blessed Lord, the Holy Virgin, and the saints; embroidering them in fine gold and seed pearls, and otherwise enriching their draperies by borderings of real and various coloured gems.

* The pall, when not in use, is also kept in the burse.

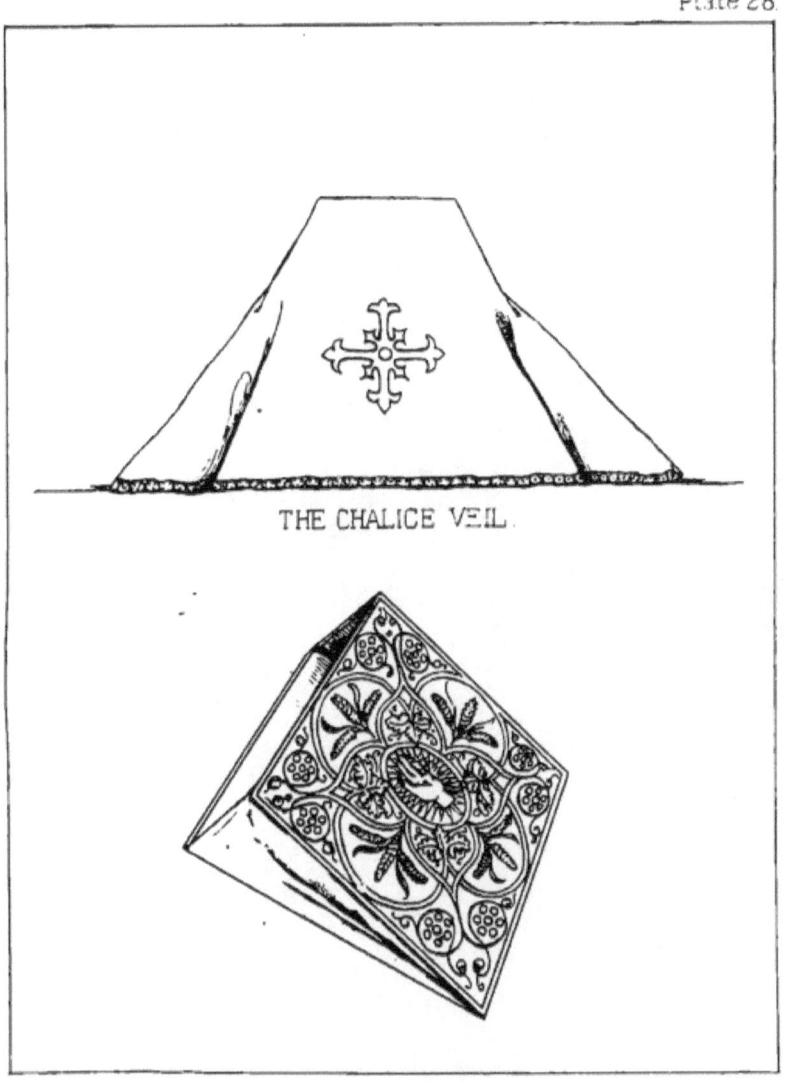

THE CHALICE VEIL.

THE BURSE.

The Burse.

Burses such as described may be recognised in most of the inventories of sacred appointments recorded by Dugdale.

The making up of the corporal case is one of the most apparently complicated operations of the Church needlewoman. To secure its perfect squareness, and neatness withal, the following is the only sure plan of proceeding :—

Two squares of tolerably stout Bristol board should be cut, to the size appointed for the burse, with such precision that they may not differ from each other even by the fiftieth part of an inch.

These are best cut out upon a board, with a sharp penknife guided by a straight-edged rule.*

Two more pieces of Bristol board must also be cut in a similar manner to the above, and of the same dimensions one way, but *one inch less* the other.

Over the two perfect squares, the upper side of the burse—that which may have the cross upon it—and the plain silk for the under side are to be stretched. Over the two curtailed squares the lawn is to be strained.

Upon the upper silk side, unless there be a needlework border, the woven lace binding is to be laid flat round the edge, and nicely mitred at the corners; holding the card, as a frame, in the hand, and passing the needle backwards and forwards through the edge of the lace, to form minute stitches on the right, and those of about half an inch long, on the wrong or cardboard side.

A gusset of silk, the length of the burse, and two inches wide at the top, and tapering to half an inch at the bottom, is to be

---

* It is quite worth the while of those who have many burses to make, to have a square cut in thin metal, which may be laid down upon the card, on a board, and held by one hand firmly, while cutting close round its sides with a sharp knife. Square after square may speedily be produced in this way, without a hair's breadth of variation.

Church Vestments.

firmly tacked to each linen division on the cardboard side; then, the two silk-covered cards are to be attached to the linen-covered pieces by sewing them against the gussets up each side, and by bringing the two cards together, and sewing them neatly along the two top edges, as well as across the bottom.

The linen cards are shortened at the bottom, that there may not be four thicknesses of card to bring together along the closed edge of the burse. On Plate 28 we have illustrated an open burse to show the gusset, and the appearance of the article when correctly made. The design is for a corporal case to be used at times of solemn Benediction of the Blessed Sacrament, when there is no Mass.

The Surplice.

XIX.

THE SURPLICE.

THIS, the most ample of all the white garments belonging to ecclesiastical dress, originated in the primitive alb, from which, in the eleventh century, it was enlarged by the Anglo-Saxon clergy, that a fur garment might be worn beneath it in cold seasons.

The word *surplice* being compounded from the Latin *super*, above, and *pellis*, a skin, or *pellicia*, a skin-vest, fully explains the first purpose of the enlarged alb; the new name for which—*surplice*—we find, does not appear in any record till the time of St. Edward the Confessor.

Dr. Rock observes that at one time in some parts of England the surplice was remarkable for having a hood attached to it, which might be drawn up and worn over the head. He also says: " The surplice was not allowed so thoroughly to supersede " the use among the lower clergy of its prototype the alb, but " what that latter garment, at the more solemn services such as " High Mass, and in great processions, was required up to the

Church Vestments.

"last day of its being in the Use which St. Osmund framed for
"Salisbury, to be worn by the younger clerks who had to wait
"more immediately around the altar, and ministered as acolytes
"and incense-bearers at the holy sacrifice.

"The spirit of St. Osmund's rubrics clearly is, that though
"the surplice might be worn by those of the clergy who sat in
"the choir, or had to move to another quarter of the church to
"sing any portion of the office, still for every one employed
"about the altar, no matter at what distance from it, and though
"even he were not more than an acolyte, the alb was the allotted
"garment: if we may so say, the surplice was the choral, the alb
"the sacrificial ministering robe."

In the Catholic Church of the present day, the celebrating priests at the Mass wear the alb beneath the chasuble, dalmatic, and tunicle, while the surplice may be assumed, alike by the preacher, the choir-boys, thurifers, and many others, who though servants of the Church may not be of the clergy.*

The surplice was worn very long, even to touch the ground, till nearly the middle of the fourteenth century. See Plates 30 and 31, extracted from Queen Mary's Psalter.

About this time—1339—we read of a constitution of Benedict the Twelfth in which it was ordered that all canons, within the choir and closes of cathedrals and other conventual places, should wear their surplices of such a size that the sleeves should extend in length, below the pendent hand, to *four* hands' breadth, and that the garment itself should be long enough "to "reach lower than the middle of the shin, or thereabouts." And further, it was at the same time ordered that outside the churches,

---

* Knyghton relates that, A.D. 1392, on the return of Richard the Second to London, he was welcomed by a grand procession, in which, walking with the bishop and clergy, were five hundred boys arrayed in surplices.

TRUE FORM OF SURPLICE. Plate 29

The Surplice.

cloisters, and places aforesaid, everywhere, and in all fitting places, the surplice might be worn by the canons, beneath their cappas and mantles, with sleeves about a Roman foot in depth, and long enough in the skirt to reach to the middle of the shin.

The ample proportions of the surplice ordered for the regular canons in the first part of this decree, are those adhered to at this moment by the promoters of a revived taste for all that is dignified and grand in vestments for the Church. And who will not go with these authorities in a preference for the beautiful, plainly-made, lawn surplice, with seams and hems so neatly sewn that stitches are only to be discovered in admiration for their regularity, to the short, unmeaning, high-shouldered garment with meagre sleeves, and bordered with paltry lace, in which some amongst the clergy, and others about the various ceremonies of the Church, are too often seen enrobed?

Quite as much to be condemned is the surplice formerly introduced from France, and happily now going out of use, which instead of sleeves has wide open pieces like wings flapping about the shoulders, and leaving the arms to display the cassock in a most unbecoming manner.

The ancient surplice had sleeves, so full and long, that the hands of the wearer could be easily enfolded within them for the protection of the service-books from undue moisture of the skin. All degrees of the clergy wore the garment of the same ample form; but according to their rank, so it differed in the quality of its material and embellishment.*

---

* Among other pious bequests, Dame Elizabeth Andrews, A.D. 1474, says :—" I will, " that Stoke Church shall have a surplice made of a piece of linen cloth containing 26 yards." And " to the church of Weston, 20 yards of linen cloth to make a surplice."—*Church of our Fathers.*

Church Vestments.

Thread embroideries of blue, and sometimes of red, were not unfrequent around the neck of the surplice of a priest; and, strange as it may appear now, we are assured, " that it was the custom in " some places in England not only for the clergy of a church to " dine together on one of the great holidays, but to sit down to " table each in his surplice."

The thurifer heading this chapter is from a scene in the life of Richard Beauchamp, Earl of Warwick, and sketched from a Cottonian MS., Julius, E. IV. The figure is shown exactly as it appears in the manuscript, where it attracted us by the near resemblance of its robe to the simple and majestic surplice of Dr. Rock, which we had previously obtained permission to copy for Plate 29, as an example of the correct shape of the garment.

The latter is made of fine lawn.

Its length; $1\frac{1}{4}$ yard, behind and before alike.

Its width at bottom, including a gore at each side of $\frac{3}{4}$ yard wide, is $5\frac{3}{4}$ yards.

These gores are $\frac{3}{4}$ of a yard deep.

The sleeves are 3 yards in circumference at bottom, and have gussets inserted of 15 inches square.

The depth of the sleeves is 1 yard at the top of the arm, and 1 yard and 7 inches deep at the longest part.

The neck is sloped round with great nicety, so that when the head is passed through, the garment arranges itself on the figure without need of fastening of any description; and being precisely the same behind and before, it is usual to work a tiny cross in blue or white cotton at the back of the neck, for the wearer's guidance in putting it on.

The chequer stitch confining the gathers is generally worked either in coarse " Boars-head " cotton, or in a fine bobbin cord. This is now the only ornament approved on the surplice.

ARCHBISHOP AND BISHOPS VESTED IN PALLIUM, CHASUBLE AND COPE.

Plate 10

PRIESTS IN SURPLICES
13th Century

The Surplice.

Indeed, excessive neatness in make, and careful washing and "getting up," are all that need be observed to render the robe fit for its good use. *Plaiting, marked* by the iron or other means, is wholly discountenanced for the surplice, which should hang naturally and gracefully over the figure, in soft and unrestrained folds.

Molinet remarks upon a kind of surplice without sleeves, which in his time—1666—was being worn in some places, and was nearly of the same circular form as the ample old chasuble. He concludes his observation of this particular surplice in the following words:—" Les chanoines reguliers de la congre-" gation de Sainte Croix de Conimbre en Portugal, quelqu'uns " d'Allemagne, et mesme de France, les portent encore decette " maniere, qui a quelque chose d'antique et de venerable."

XX.

THE COTTA.

THE Cotta, a garment worn at the altar services in some churches by the assistant priests and acolytes, is nothing more than a very poor substitute for the ample surplice.

As the latter is really the only correct white robe to be worn over the cassock by all servitors at the altar, save those wearing the sacrificial vestments, from the tonsured priest to the smallest choir-boy, we do not feel it incumbent upon us to describe the short, undignified appurtenance called the cotta.

Setting aside its mean appearance, nowhere do we find any authority for its adoption.

We have alluded to the cotta as being worn by certain officials at the Ecclesiastical Court of Rome, but we can take no precedent from such a source for our, sometimes, indiscriminate use of the garment to the exclusion of the surplice.

On Plate 33, we give two, *not* exaggerated, examples of the cotta, as we have so frequently seen it in France.

Fig. 1 is the crimped cotta.

Fig. 2, the crochet cotta.

Corporal-Cloths.

XXI.

THE SACRED LINEN OF THE ALTAR — CORPORAL-CLOTHS, PALLS, PURIFICATORS, AND LAVABOR-TOWELS.

IT is possible that a description of the above may not be looked for among vestments, nevertheless, we do not withhold it, as information upon the subject may prove useful to some of our readers.

In "Church Embroidery," the corporal-cloth is mentioned with a view to its ornamentation only, and the pall is glanced at, in the same place, in a manner so confusing, that we are constrained to make the present work the medium of an apology for the oversight, which has allowed, what may be construed into an error, to appear under our name.

The above-mentioned book was printed, and bound, before we discovered the two little words, which from being misread in our manuscript, and strangely overlooked in our correction of the proofs, left us responsible for erroneously representing the corporal-cloth to be one and the same, at the present day, as the pall.

It is perfectly true, nevertheless, that formerly the corporal-cloth was made large enough to spread the whole way along the top of the altar, and that one end of it was frequently used to cover the chalice, as a pall—a custom continued in many of the principal churches in France up to a very late period.

Church Vestments.

In Strutt's "Regal Antiquities," Plate 28, where the Earl of Northumberland is shown at an altar taking an oath of fealty to King Richard, the corporal-cloth upon which the noble is swearing* is opened out upon the middle of the altar, with one end shrouding the chalice.

The origin of the large corporal, which overspread the top of the altar, may be traced to the days when the true followers of the faith, being rigid observers of the rites of the Church, were zealous frequenters of the Blessed Sacrament; and the altar-breads for such numerous communicants were all laid out, and consecrated upon this especial cloth.

Upon the corporal, also, were the offerings deposited after the Credo; in commemoration of which usage the deacon now, as of old, at the conclusion of the "Et Incarnatus est," advances to the credence-table, and from thence to the altar, bearing with him the burse containing the corporal. This he spreads upon the altar, and then returns to resume his seat at the side of the priest till the end of the Credo.

As the Blessed Host is now no longer, as formerly, reserved only for the sick, but is kept ready for all who may present themselves for Communion at the Holy Mass, the large corporal has fallen into disuse, and a cloth seldom more than 20 inches square supplies its place.

According to the Roman Catholic Ritual, the corporal should be of finest linen, and its decoration chaste and simple.† A small cross worked in the centre, in white or in red cotton, is

---

* This is the interpretation of the "Corporal-oath," of which we read in the middle ages.

† Although it would seem from the following, extracted from an old inventory of the sacred possessions of St. George's Chapel, Windsor, that the corporal was once more richly ornamented :—

"Item, undecim corporalia, quorum, unum magnum pro majore calice aureâ, cum repo-
"sitorio bono, ornato cum perlis.

"Item, unum de ale, et unum de ravidale."

Plate 31

ACOLYTES SURPLICES FROM QUEEN MARY'S PSALTER.

The Purificator.

often its only ornament. Crosses may also be embroidered in the four corners.

Both corporal-cloth and pall, being solemnly blessed for the most sacred service of the Holy Eucharist, after they have been used, may not be touched by one of the laity until they have been first washed by a clerk in Holy Orders. The same injunction applies to the purificator.

The pall is the small square used for covering the chalice. It is usually made of finest linen or lawn, with a piece of thin card placed between the doubled material. Its size varies from $4\frac{1}{2}$ to 6 inches. It should have a cross embroidered in the centre in white cotton, and may also have one worked in each corner. The most correct finish for the edge is a hem of a quarter of an inch wide, turned over on the right side, and neatly stitched.

In churches where the Roman rite is strictly followed, the cardboard is dispensed with for the pall, and the required firmness gained, by stiffly starching the doubled linen. The Roman pall, too, is little more than 4 inches square, and invariably bordered by a lace of about an inch and a half wide.

The *Purificator*, or *Mundatory*, is the linen napkin used for wiping the sacred vessels at the Holy Mass.

It is sometimes made square, and about 14 inches in size. An oblong square, however, is that to which we find the most favour shown by the clergy. The purificators employed at St. George's Cathedral measure 17 by 10 inches. They should be made of pure fine lawn, and be very neatly hemmed.

A small cross in red cotton is usually worked in the centre of this napkin. Crosses may also be worked in the corners, but they should be of a simple kind.

The purificator required at the Communion of the Sick,

should be 9 inches square, and marked with a cross in the centre.

The lavabor towel is that upon which the priest wipes his fingers during the oblation of the Holy Mass.

We find a general objection to these towels being large, although Gavantus directed that they should measure one yard long and ¾ of a yard wide.

Those in use at St. George's Cathedral average 18 by 14 inches, and are made of the very finest diaper, and simply hemmed round.

The Credence Cloth.

The Credence is the table which stands at the south side of the altar, to bear the sacred vessels, and other special appointments appertaining to the Holy Eucharist.

This table is always covered with a pure white cloth, which should either hang down at each side to touch the ground, or fall over to the depth of 5 inches, as along the front.

In many churches the credence-cloth is as handsomely ornamented as that of the altar itself: this is unnecessary. It should have a hem of an inch wide, and above it may be a narrow border worked in chain-stitch, with red and white cotton.

XXII.

THE CANON'S COPE.

THE Canon's Cope was a large plain cloak reaching to the feet, always black, and made of thin cloth or other woollen material. It was open, nearly, from the waist downwards, but permanently closed above, so that it had to be put on over the head. A hood was also attached to it, but this was seldom worn up, as the *furred amys* was made to answer all purposes of protection, from cold, about the head and shoulders.

Both grades of the clergy, in the cathedral and collegiate churches, wore over the cassock, for the services of the choir, at an early period, the alb—subsequently the surplice; but the canon's black cope was always the upper garment in which they came "by night as at matins, and by day, for prime, tierce, "sext, and none; or, as they are called, the 'little hours.'"

Only on high festivals and Saints' days was the black cope laid aside to exhibit the pure white alb, or the surplice, or to assume the still more jubilant robe, the rich silk cope of the colour of the day, in which the wearer was to swell the glorious procession, and to do honour to the grand High Mass.

A black woollen cloak, closely resembling the canon's cope of former days, is still worn at certain offices of the Church, by some orders of priests.

Church Vestments.

XXIII.

THE FURRED AMYS.

THE Furred Amys, anciently called the "almucia," was always worn with the canon's black cope; and we can suppose that in inclement seasons of the year, at night, and in early morning, when the clergy pursued their divine offices in the choir, it must have been held a most grateful addition to the thin cloth cloak.

Like the canon's cope, the exterior material of the amys was usually of a black woollen fabric, but, inside, it was lined with fur—the quality of which was proportionate to the rank and degree of the wearer, in the church and the choir; and pendent from the lower hem, about the shoulders, fastened like a fringe, were the tails of the animals of whose fur the lining was made.

The "amictus ex grisia" was the amys made of a costly fur of a silver-grey shade, and which was worn only by canons of the highest class, while that of the minor canon was constructed of a skin called *Calabrian*, from the Italian province where the animal supplying the fur was principally found. We find that the *grey amys* was, "as a mark of honour, allowed to the royal "chaplains;" and as one proof of this are told that at the funeral Mass of Henry the Seventh, "After the lords and barrons had "made theire offeringe, then followed the chapleins of dignitie "and the *grey amezes* of the King's chappell" (Leland's "Col-"lectanea," vol. iii., p. 308). By the same chronicler, at the christening of Prince Arthur, eldest son of Henry the Seventh,

The Furred Amys

"many noble doctors in riche copes and *grey amys*" are described as being present.

By the beginning of the fourteenth century, the furred amys was not so much in requisition, as a head-covering, as heretofore, for a small round cap began to be preferred, and was allowed to be worn, by the clergy, at certain parts of the Divine service. Then, the amys was left to fall behind as a hood, and to secure it about the neck it was necessary to close the two corresponding sides of the front together, so that in putting it on, the head had to be passed through the opening. After this, the amys took the form of a cape or tippet; still the hood was not relinquished, but hung around the neck, to be used, doubtless, as occasion might require.

It also kept its fringe of tails, and in addition were attached to its cape-like ends in front, two straight narrow strips of fur, which hung down even below the knees, and in some representations of ecclesiastical figures of the period may well be mistaken for the stole. Early in the sixteenth century the amys had got to be shaped like a small shawl, deeper behind than before, with the two strips of fur still attached to it in front, but no longer straight; they were very wide where they joined the ends of the cape, and tapered off to a mere point at their extremities.

By this time, too, what was originally the outside of the garment had become the lining, and the fur the only material rendered visible. The semblance of a hood seems to have been all that the amys retained of its original design as a head-covering, and this it kept to its very last days.

The following interesting passage from the "Church of our "Fathers," may fitly close our account of the ancient amys:—

"Doctors of divinity and dignitaries in the Protestant Esta-

Church Vestments.

"blishment of England, still keep up the use of the scarlet
"gown in the universities on solemn occasions,* and the daily
"wear of the scarlet hood hanging behind from the shoulders in
"the cathedrals. This, to my thinking, is not the old, but a
"modern way of putting it on: anciently, the doctor's hood
"was placed upon his shoulders, and not behind, as is shown
"from the ceremonial of our Catholic Kings at the feast of the
"Epiphany, as is instanced in Henry the Seventh, who, on the
"'twelfth even, went to the evensong in his surcoot outward,
"with taber sleeves, the cappe of estate on his hede, and the
"hode aboute his showlders in doctors wise.'"

* Anciently, "Doctors in divinity or canon-law might be at once recognised by a scarlet "amys furred with grey; the full canon had assigned him one that was outside black, but "within made of the same fine grey skins, of a deep silvery hue; while to every person "beneath that rank it was forbidden, with a few exceptions, to have any other than a dark "brown and cheaper kind of fur in this article of Church attire."—*Church of Our Fathers.*

The Mitre.

XXIV.

THE MITRE.

TO the Mitre could be assigned a very early origin, might we be certain that the plate of gold which Eusebius tells us St. John the Evangelist wore upon his forehead, was to denote his rank among the Christian priests of his time; or, that the like ornament ascribed by Epiphanius to St. James, was equally indicative of that apostle's high vocation in his Divine Master's service.

We may, however, be justified in holding it quite within the range of probability, that such distinguishing marks of head-attire were assumed by these holy men in honour of a spiritual, rather than a temporal cause; for, it would be little short of blasphemy to suppose that a desire for worldly display could have caused them thus to adorn themselves.

Eminent liturgical writers have proved that, long before the sixth century, a golden crown, set with gems, was the most prominent feature of the bishop's insignia; and that even abbots at a somewhat later period wore a jewelled band, which encircled the forehead nearly to the eyebrows. The figure of St. Benedict, pictured in St. Ethelwold's Benedictional, shows this ornament, on the head of the saint, most perfectly.

Fig. 1, Plate 36, was sketched from the above.

For many centuries after the sixth, not only in England but in Italy, and, in short, in every place on the Continent where

Church Vestments.

Christianity was known, was this golden diadem peculiar to the episcopacy. It is even said that it was not abandoned as late as the twelfth century.

But, as well as this jewelled coronal, a kind of linen head-dress was worn by Anglo-Saxon prelates of the eighth century; it was made of the finest flaxen cloth, and bound flat to the head by two strips of the same material, which were secured behind, and their long ends left to fall about the shoulders. Over this was placed the ornamental band.

At a subsequent period, the bishop's *head-linen*, as we find it called, was worn without crown or other dignified accompaniment whatever.

It was about the end of the tenth century when the mitre took its first definite form, insomuch as it was shaped something like a rather high skull-cap, with pendants from the back, commemorative of the *infulæ*, or lappets, of the ancient head-linen.

In, or about, the time of Edward the Confessor, the sides of the mitre were elevated to two short horns, or points, with a slight depression or curve extending from one to the other, along the top. Fig. 2, Plate 36, may convey some idea of this shape.

Fig. 3, on the same Plate, illustrates the mitre, from twelfth-century examples, after its next change, with the points lowered and rounded off. This form could not have obtained long, for with its date we find one nearly coeval, given to the introduction of what we may safely call the established type of the Catholic bishop's mitre, viz., that split open at top, and with back and front elevations sloping towards the now depressed sides. This is well exhibited on Plates 6 and 30.

No variation of any importance can be traced in the actual

The Mitre.

shape of the mitre from the twelfth to the end of the fifteenth century. It went through this period increasing in beauty and costliness of decoration, till the skill of the embroiderer was taxed to the uttermost point of perfection, and the manipulative art of the goldsmith came to a stand-still, as if puzzled to produce anything more exquisite than the Limerick mitre, with its mine of priceless gems, and its deftly crocketed sides. But still, those striking peculiarities, which made the mitre different to every other form of either sacred or secular head-covering, remained the same.

It was early in the sixteenth century, when the mitre began, literally, to grow out of the simplicity of its dignified old shape,* for it gradually increased in height, and became more and more smooth and bulged at the sides, until the middle of the eighteenth century, when it no longer presented an article of ecclesiastical costume suggestive of reverence, but an ungainly head-encumbrance, anything but uniform with the solemnity of the episcopal degree.

Such a mitre is exhibited in fig. 4, on Plate 36.

Till within the last twenty-five years, this form of mitre endured. It was still in vogue when the late Pugin wrote, in 1844, but, thanks to the zealous, untiring spirit of that great reviver of all that was best in the ecclesiastical ornament of the middle ages, the bishop's head-covering, in symmetry and embellishment, is once more worthy of its purpose. For, at this moment, the mitre of the Catholic prelate is strictly ordered to be made, nearly as may be, to that of the fourteenth century. A perfect example of which exists for us on the figure of Thomas de la Mare, shown on Plate 11.

* The mitre of William of Wykeham—fourteenth century—is only 10 inches high; that of Bishop O'Deagh, the Limerick mitre, 13 inches; while the ordinary height of the mitre in the sixteenth century was 18 inches.

Church Vestments.

Every bishop now, as anciently, has three kinds of mitre, to be worn on different occasions.

1. The Simplex, of plain white linen, which may be, as it is often, made of white silk, with no ornament whatever.

2. The Auriphrygiata, adorned with gold orphreys and needlework.

3. The Pretiosa, the mitre embellished with jewels, pearls, and enamels, and in every way precious from the wealth of rare materials and the work of well-skilled hands.

The mitre of St. Thomas of Canterbury, with which all must be familiar, clearly illustrates that called the "mitra auri-"phrygiata." The exquisite proportions and true harmony of the scroll-work, spread over its head-piece and pendants, are a feast to the eyes. The ornament on its orphreys is that wonderfully ancient and mysterious figure called the *gammadion*, from its representation of the Greek letter *gamma*, four times repeated.

Waller, whom Pugin in some part took for his authority, in remarking upon this singular device, says that it was known and used, in India and China, ten centuries before Christ, by a sect styling themselves "doctors of reason, and followers of the mystic "cross." Subsequently it was adopted by the worshippers of Buddha, full six hundred years in advance of the Saviour, and is to be met with on most of the Buddhist coins and inscriptions found throughout India.

The "gammadion" is supposed to have been brought into Christendom at a very early period. Waller says, probably, it came among us about the sixth century; Pugin proves its existence in the paintings of the Roman catacombs long before, by signalizing the figure of a *fossor*, or excavator, buried there, named Diogenes, who has this ornament figured on his habit, and whose monument is certainly not later than the third century.

It is said that in Thibet the Nestorians used the "gammadion" as an emblem of "God crucified for the salvation of the human "race." If all, or only a part of such accounts as this, which are handed down to us, of the religious antiquity of the device, be true, we may indeed hold as most mystical the ornament which, in Pugin's words, was "not only in use among the Christians "from primitive times, but prophetically borne for centuries "before the coming of our Lord."

In the Sanscrit language "swastica" is said to be the term for the gammadion; in heraldry it is known as the *fylfot*. Waller, in his "Monumental Brasses," speaks of the fylfot as being depicted on the arms of some Yorkshire families, in a manuscript of the fourteenth century, and we have ourselves seen it on military effigies of the middle ages.

The pattern exhibited upon the miniature preaching stole, Plate 34, is the "gammadion" copied literally from the finely-vested effigy of an ecclesiastic, figured in Shaw's "Dresses and "Decorations of the Middle Ages," from an incised slab of the fourteenth century, brought from the abbey of St. Genevieve, and now affixed to the wall in the exterior court of the Palais des Beaux Arts, at Paris.

The engraving on our title-page illustrates the "gammadion" and quatrefoil, alternated in squares, as frequently represented in the early decorative period.

Like the sacred vestment of the illustrious martyr, the mitre of St. Thomas of Canterbury has been the model in these latter days of the revival of mediæval art, not only for mitres, but for ornament upon secular as well as sacred things. Its elegant scroll pattern has been imitated and used in endless different

Church Vestments.

ways. It has been fashioned into borders for linen altar-cloths;* its graceful lines have adorned the skirt of the alb; and it has been worked in every variety of material, from the precious metals to worsted, for ante-pendia and altar-carpets.

Then, without the Church, architect and decorator have alike had it in request for iron railings, fret-work carving, and cornice-painting; albeit, that we have sometimes remarked more taste in the recognition of a good design, than judgment in the selection of an appropriate one.

The pattern upon the mitre in question is embroidered principally in gold, couched upon a white ground, which is of an elaborate diaper pattern. Red is introduced in the orphreys, and a little bright blue in the "gammadion:" it is without gems or gold ornament of any kind. Hence, it is called the "mitra "auriphrygiata." Among the few examples left of the "mitra "pretiosa," we may number that of William of Wykeham, enough of which still remains to prove how rich it was, originally, in gold, jewels, pearls, and enamels.

The Limerick mitre illustrated by Shaw, is a lovely specimen of the jewelled mitre, being made at the very beginning of the fifteenth century, when ecclesiastical handiwork of all kinds was luxuriant with ornamental detail. Its construction is described as of "thin solid plates of silver, studded with precious "stones."

In the inventory, given in to Henry the Eighth, of Winchester Monastery, the following items occur:—

"Item—Three standing† mitres, silver and gilt, garnished with "pearls and precious stones.

---
* *Vide* Plate 16 of Pugin's Glossary.
† *Standing mitres* were those formed of thin, but solid sheets of gold or silver.

The Mitre.

"Item—Ten old mitres, garnished with pearls and precious "stones after the old fashion."*

Mitres of this particular kind are also put down in an inventory, of a very early date, of the vestiary possessions of St. George's Chapel, Windsor. Two are thus mentioned:—

"Item mitra bona, ornata lapidibus pretiosis.

"Item una mitra bona, cum diversis lapidibus, in qûa deficiunt "tres lapides."

The ground-work of the ancient mitre, judging from the remnants of such as have been preserved, seems always to have been white. No matter whether the foundation was of silk, silver, or of seed-pearls, white was evidently held more correct than colour, to represent the main portion of this episcopal attire.

In the "Church of our Fathers" the following is said relative to the use of the mitre according to the Roman Ritual:—

"In the Ordo Romanus XIII., drawn up by command of "Pope Gregory Xth, A.D. 1271, the white colour of the mitre "and its three kinds, plain and enriched, according to the feast- "day upon which each had to be worn, is clearly laid down:— "Dominus Papa tres mitras diversas habet, quibus diversis tem- "poribus utitur; scilicet unam albam totam, unam cum auri- "frisio in titulo sine circulo, et mitram aurifrisiatum in circulo et "in titulo. Mitra aurifrisiata in circulo et in titulo utitur in "officiis diebris festis et aliis. . . . Mitra vero cum aurifrisio in "titulo sine circulo, utitur cum sedet in consistorio. . . . . . Alba "utitur diebus dominicis et aliis non festivis."

The word *titulus* is explained as the "stripe of gold running "up the middle of the mitre."

---

* *Mitres after the old fashion*, were those of parchment foundations, covered with white silk, or a web of small seed pearls.

Church Vestments.

An archbishop's mitre from a sculptured figure, probably of the thirteenth century, from one of the portals of Chartres Cathedral, is shown in fig. 6, Plate 36.

This is a rare example of its kind, and will be seen to bear a near resemblance, in outline, to a Pope's mitre from Queen Mary's Psalter, illustrated by fig. 5, on the same Plate.

The latter appears with the first of the three crowns which now compose the tiara of the Pontiff. Pope Boniface the Eighth, at the end of the thirteenth century, adopted the second crown; and Urban the Fifth, A.D. 1334, added the third and final coronet.

The Pope only assumes the tiara on the most solemn ceremonies, such as that of the "Urbi et Orbi," etc. At the celebration of the Holy Mass at Christmas, Easter, and other great festivals, he wears a mitre. The tiara presented by the Queen of Spain to Pope Pius the Ninth is said to have cost 80,000*l*.

There is no better foundation or stiffener for the *simple* and *orphreyed* mitres than that which was used for the purpose in ancient times, viz., parchment; and, whether the mitre be of plain linen, ornamented, or precious, it has to be made to fit the head of the wearer, as any hat or cap.

A band of leather, of full 4 inches deep, should be sewn around it inside, and the lining carried up to the height of the straight, upright sides. The lining of the outside, to lie properly between the cleft, is cut separately, and attached to the outside, after the inside has been made complete. It is usually cut of a lozenge shape, of sides equal to those of the triangle described at the upper part of the mitre, and is sewn by its four even sides to those of the triangular opening. Over these seams in ornamented mitres a cord may be placed; but the plain white linen mitre is neatly sewn together, and that is all.

The Mitre.

A beautiful mitra simplex, of ancient form, in modern use, is before us.

It is of purest white linen, also its pendants; its only decoration the even stitches by which it has been put together.

From the base to the topmost point it measures 13 inches. Across the base of the triangle, 13 inches. From the base of the triangle to its apex, 8½ inches. Sides of triangle, 11 inches.

The pendants are 13 inches long, and tapering from 3½ inches wide at the lowermost end, to 2½ inches at the upper extremity, where they are attached to the mitre at a distance of 2½ inches apart.

The following instructive passage relating to the setting of gems in the "mitra pretiosa," may be welcome to some of our readers, who have not ready access to the work from which it is extracted:—*

"Precious stones on a mitre, a hallowed vessel, or in anything
"for the house of God, should not be cut, as ladies' jewels are, in
"facets, but *en cabochon*, that is, in the unbroken, pebble-like
"shape. Apart from the difference which ought always to dis-
"tinguish the sacred from the secular, even in ornament, there
"is greater broadness of colour and depth of tint, a something
"grander, in gems when set in smooth elliptical form. The
"jewels upon every kind of church ornament were invariably
"mounted *en cabochon* during the mediæval period."

* "The Church of our Fathers."

XXV.

THE ROCHET.

THE Rochet, now worn only by prelates, is best described as a very short alb, in which garment, like the surplice, it claims its origin. Its sleeves are narrower than those of the alb; but with this exception, and that of its inferior length, it differs in no respect from that robe.

Molinet, writing in 1666, after describing the form of the rochet, says:—" Ils appellait autrefois *tunica linea*, et l'usage en
" estoit seulement permis dans les monasteres de l'ordre, aux
" officiers, et à ceux qui travoilloient, et etoient employés aux
" ouvrages de la maison, comme nous l'aprenons des Consti-
" tutoîs de Sainte Geneniefue, au chapitre de vestiaris cy-devant
" allegué, *si operarius sit, tunicam lineam habere poterit;* on
" remarque aussi dans le chapitre de *labore fratrum*, du mesme
" livre, que tous les religieux en prenoient pour aller au travail.
" Enfin la commodité a introduit la coûtume dans le ordre de se
" servir de ces tuniques de linge, ou rochets pour l'habit ordi-
" naire et de revestir se surplis par dessus, pour assister à l'Office
" Divin; afin sans doute que le surplis ne servant plus qu'à
" l'Eglise, fut plus blanc et plus honneste. L'usage de ce
" rochet etoit desia commu parmy les chanoines reguliers, en
" 1340, puis qu'il en est fait mention dans les constitutions de
" Benoist XII., ou il les appelle, *superpellicium ad formam*
" *rochettorum seu camisiarium Romanorum.*"

Plate 32.

THE ROCHET

The Rochet.

That the alb was worn over the rochet, for the celebration of the Mass, in the thirteenth century we find from a canon of the Church of Liege, A.D. 1287, which orders "that priests wear " under their albs either a surplice, or the linen tunic generally " known as the rochet." From other authorities we gather, that up to the period just named the *tunica linea* was synonymous with the surplice; but it would seem that, by the time this decree was enacted, the rochet had obtained recognition, as a garment distinct from the full, wide-sleeved surplice, the very amplitude of which would prevent its being worn beneath the alb. It is said by some writers that on this account the rochet was primitively used without sleeves; an assertion which may be reasonably entertained, when we reflect on the incapability of the narrow sleeves of the alb, to contain any amount of bulk without producing an awkward and ungraceful effect, such as we may look in vain for, in any article of the ecclesiastical dress of the middle ages.

Molinet has shown us in his "Figures des differents Habits " des Chanoines Reguliers," the work just quoted from, how the rochet came into favour with the regular canons; and we find also from various ancient inventories how the custom of wearing this diminished form of alb became general; and that the assumption of it was allowed to servants of inferior degree in the Church, such as cantors and choir children.*

This last is clearly proved in the following extract from Dugdale, from the inventory of St. Mary Hill, London :—

---

* "This did not hinder the rochet, properly so called, from being looked upon as a " garment especially belonging to the episcopal vesture; for while but a priest, our country- " man Richard de Bury, who afterwards filled the see of Durham so worthily, had given " him, by the hands of the Roman pontiff, a rochet, for a pledge that the Holy See would " name him to the very first bishopric which might become vacant in England."—*Church of our Fathers.*

Church Vestments.

"Item, 8 surplyces for the quere.
"Item, 3 *rochets* for children.
"Item, 3 albys for children, with parells."

By the mention of surplices and albs in the same list with the rochets, we are at once assured that by this time the latter was a garment as distinguished from the surplice, and alb, as they were from each other.

Only prelates, and canons regular, as heretofore, now assume the rochet.

It is the robe worn on ordinary occasions by the Holy Father himself, over his white *soutane*, or cassock, and beneath his ermine-bordered mozetta.

In grand processions cardinal-bishops carry the rochet over their cassocks, and the cope above.

So likewise is the rochet borne by cardinal-priests, and deacons, beneath the chasuble and the dalmatic; and, again, by cardinals of the Papal choir, when in grand costume, it is put on over the cassock, to be surmounted by that majestic robe called the *cappa-magna;* while above all is placed the mozetta, which is of silk in summer, and entirely of ermine in the winter.

The four masters of the ecclesiastical ceremonies of the Court of Rome wear over their violet cassocks, first the rochet, and above that a less deep garment, called a *cotta*, with short and somewhat full sleeves, descending only to the elbow.

As in nearly every case, here, as in Rome, the rochet is bordered with *lace*, and ornamented with the same material at the wrists, the cotta, when worn above it, as just mentioned, is trimmed correspondingly, and its short sleeves frequently formed altogether by a fall of lace.

It may be needless to remark that the lace thus employed for either rochet or cotta should be, as we admit it often is, of the

The Rochet.

richest and rarest kind ; and, if possible, it should be that made in convents or other Catholic establishments, where the dignity of the Church is respected, and the appointments of her ministers held too sacred, to be mixed up with secular ideas of dress and ornament.

Were this made a rule, and one strictly followed in the ordering of all fitting things for the sacerdotal office, the beautiful solemnities of the Church would be rendered more impressive, and our ears happily saved from so much profane talk about *Church millinery.*

The example of the rochet given on Plate 32 is the most simple and correct we have met with in our research. The figure is taken from Molinet's work, where it is shown to represent the dress of a regular canon of the Abbey de Saint Jean de Chartres.

Church Vestments.

XXVI.

THE SUBCINGULUM.

THE *Subcingulum* is now worn, only, by the Roman Pontiff when vested for the celebration of Mass on solemn occasions, and has the appearance of a maniple suspended from the left side of the girdle.

This appendage seems to have originated in a belt, or second binding for the waist of the alb; for we find, early in the ninth century, that every bishop was ordered to wear it over his girdle, reciting a separate prayer as he assumed each of the two articles. The use of the "subcingulum" was not confined exclusively to prelates in some countries, the rubrics of which, seem to have enjoined that it should be worn by every celebrant of the solemn High Mass.*

It was about the end of the twelfth century when Pope Innocent the Third decreed that this ornament should be " ranked " among vestments allotted to the exclusive use of the episcopal " order."

---

* " No vain delay hath crossed thy way,
   " God's service needs thine aid !
   " So thought the ready page, and now
   " The sacristan he played.

   " In stole, and *cingulum* full fair,
   " He robed the priest, and went
   " The hallowed vessels to prepare
   " For God's pure sacrament."
                    SCHILLER'S *Fridolin*.

The Subcingulum.

As late as the sixteenth century, the "subcingulum" appears to have been worn by some English as well as foreign bishops, but now, as Dr. Rock observes, "it is used in the Latin Church "by the Pope only." And, he continues, "I cannot help "thinking but these two appendages were shaped like and "served as pockets. Cencio de Sabellis, the Roman Chamber-"lain, in the 'Ordo Romanus' which he drew up towards the "twelfth century, tells us that in those days when a newly-chosen "pope took solemn possession of his Cathedral Church of St. "John Lateran, 'he was girt with a belt of crimson silk, hanging "from which there was a purse, which had in it twelve precious "stones and some musk: the belt was meant to signify continence "and chastity; the purse, almsgiving to the widows, and the "needy ones of Christ; the twelve stones, the power of the "apostles; the musk, a good odour in the sight of God.'"

The subjoined concluding particulars, which we also borrow from the "Church of our Fathers," of this curious old sacerdotal ornament, are too interesting to be passed over, and too precious to be handled in the way of gleaning, we therefore give them nearly as possible in the writer's own words:—

"In the year 1224 was found the body, if not of St. Birinus, "at least of some Anglo-Saxon bishop, and among other vest-"ments upon it was a 'pera,' or gold woven purse, such as "noticed by Cencio—a pocket hung from a girdle and worn by "the saint when solemnly arrayed. Thus affording presumptive "proof that, in Anglo-Saxon times, the bishops of this country "wore, at great functions, a 'subcingulum' with its appendages, "for the same symbolic reasons as those assigned by the writers "already quoted.

"I suspect, too, that the 'duo pendentia cum aurifrisio,' sur-"rendered among so many other beautiful Anglo-Saxon vest-

Church Vestments.

" ments of Ely Church to the Norman pillagers sent round by
" William, were the pendants of an episcopal belt.

" A slight change, it would seem, was, after the pontificate of
" Innocent the Third, made in the 'subcingulum;' for when
" Durandus wrote, A.D. 1286, instead of two, it had hanging to
" it but one pocket or appendage, which was double, and on the
" left-hand side, as it is now worn by the Pope. From the near
" resemblance which this appendage, or 'succinctorium,' in its
" altered form bore to a maniple, it began, some years after the
" time of Durandus, to be called by that name.

" In an 'Ordo Missæ Pontificalis,' published by Georgi from
" a Vatican manuscript of the end of the fourteenth century, it is
" so named: 'Et primo induit (pontifex) sibi albam, deinde
" cinctorium cum manipulo ad sinistram partem.'—*Liturgia*
" *Rom. Pont.*, tom. iii., p. 556."

The Gremiale, or Lap-Cloth.

XXVII.

THE GREMIALE, OR LAP-CLOTH.

SO called from the Latin word *gremium*, was once used alike by prelate, priest, deacon, and sub-deacon, to cover the knees while seated during particular parts of the High Mass, but is now only adopted, at the Holy Service, by the bishop.

Originally, the specific object of the gremiale was to preserve the vestment from any soil or stain which might be imparted to it from the hands, which the priest, the whole time he is in a sitting posture in the sanctuary, keeps reverentially outspread upon his knees.

At this day the lap-cloth is not an unimportant article in the vestiary appointments of the bishop, for it effectually protects his robes from the incense which might sprinkle over them, as, while seated, he serves it from the boat to the thurifer.

The gremiale, at its first adoption, was, literally, a napkin of linen, supposed to be the "mellium" we read of in old records. By degrees, embroidered ornament was bestowed upon it, and that of the celebrant was, we are led to believe, distinguished from those of the assistant priests by gold, and other enriching properties. It then was formed of silk, and still further embellished; and finally, was made of the same materials as, and worked to correspond with, the different sets of officiating vestments to be worn on particular days.

The gremiale of the bishop must accord with his vestments, in

Church Vestments.

colour and style of ornament. It should be edged with a border of gold embroidery, or with a real gold lace, beyond which may be a narrow gold fringe.

The most approved size of the gremiale is a square of 34 inches.

CROSSES FOR PREACHING & OTHER STOLES

XXVIII.

THE CAPPA MAGNA.

THE word *cappa* actually bears reference to a hood, and, anciently, was so used to designate such an appurtenance, whether worn by priests or laity. *Cappa* was the term employed for the hood of the chasuble, and especially for that of the white vestment worn at the Easter celebration.

After the ordinary processional cope had become fully recognised as a clerical garment, a cloak, of larger dimensions and richer decoration, but with an available hood like its prototype, was assumed by some degrees of the clergy. This was called the Cappa Magna.

Such is the title now bestowed on that ample robe with majestic train worn in the Catholic Church by the Sovereign Pontiff, cardinals, and other high dignitaries, in choir, and at certain times of ceremony.

The cappa magna is always of the same colour as the cassock over which it is worn.

It is in this grand robe, with its train full and flowing, that the cardinal advances and pays his obedience to the Pope. As he is retiring to his place, his assistant chaplains, to accelerate his dignified progress through the crowd, roll the train of his cappa up so rapidly and ingeniously, that the movement, save to one who may be watching for it, is scarcely perceptible.

Church Vestments.

The cappa magna of the cardinal, in choir, is of the wonderful rosy-scarlet shade, excepting on Vigils, and during the greater part of Lent and Advent, when it is of violet.

Here, in England, bishops of the Church of Rome wear the violet cappa magna at certain times and seasons, such as at Tenebræ in Holy Week, etc.

The Mozetta.

XXIX.

THE MOZETTA.

THE Mozetta is the cape worn by the Pope, cardinals, and bishops, over the rochet. It is also, always put on over the cappa magna, and, used thus, is either of white fur or silk, according to the season.

His Holiness holds his receptions sitting, robed in the white cassock and rochet, surmounted by a red mozetta, bordered with ermine, and about his neck a gold-embroidered stole, caught together, but not crossed, upon his breast. At such times, too, the Pontiff wears the white, instead of the scarlet, calotte, or skull-cap.

The mozetta worn by canons in choir is black.

That of the bishop can only be of violet.

The cardinal assumes red, excepting at penitential times, when violet is used.

The shape of the silk mozetta is well shown on the sketch of an English archbishop, Plate 37.

Church Vestments.

XXX.

THE BUSKINS.

THESE, the ornamented *footed*-leggings worn by the celebrating bishop, are to be recognised in ancient documents under the title of *campagi;* at a later period they are called *caligæ*, and are still known by that name, although more generally as the buskins.

Some of the early liturgical writers might create a degree of confusion in our minds, by making *buskins* and *sandals* appear to have been synonymous, but for more recent labourers in the field of antiquity, who have compared these ambiguous accounts with others more lucid, and equally reliable, to deduce the fact, that the *buskins* and *sandals* were always distinct, as articles of pontifical vesture.

We read of a document which, A.D. 666, mentions the campagi as only to be used by the Sovereign Pontiff. Afterwards, the right of wearing them was granted to the clergy of Rome; and, finally, they became a part of the ministerial dress of every bishop.

Although originally the buskins were, no doubt, made of linen, yet very early in the tenth century it would seem that they were not only in general use among the episcopal clergy, but were of costly material and decoration; insomuch as Riculfus Helenensis thought his *caligi* and sandals, with other valuables

The Buskins.

of sacred character, a fitting bequest to a church, "for the use "of all future bishops of that see."

Long prior to the dawn of the eleventh century the embroidered stockings, or buskins, were an essential part of the bishop's pontificals, and ever since have remained so.

We have no lack of authority for the use of the buskins after the above period, since nearly every old inventory which is open to us has some record of the caligæ.

In that of Salisbury, made A.D. 1222, they are particularly mentioned; also, in the list of St. Paul's, London, A.D. 1295, where they are set down as ornamented in the richest manner.

The episcopal stocking of Bishop Waneflete, illustrated by Dr. Rock, in his "Church of our Fathers," may justly be considered an unique example of the bishop's buskin at its most advanced stage of embellishment.

It is described as "of cloth of silver, embroidered with birds "in gold, with flowers in coloured silks, and with sun-rays "darting from a cloud, seemingly the device of Edward the "Fourth."

This buskin, with the prelate's sandal, shown on Plate 36, is kept in St. Mary Magdalen College, at Oxford.

The buskins are the first articles of sacred attire put on by the bishop when robing for the Mass. They are now, as the sandals, usually made of lama, and always of the colour of the day.

To decorate them with embroidery is optional: most of those used in England are of the rich unfigured lama. Their shape is precisely like a very wide stocking, made to reach just above the knees, where they are tied by strings of ribbon run through a hem, that the top of the buskin may be drawn up to the size of the leg.

The bishop puts off his ordinary shoes to assume the buskins,

Church Vestments.

and, as he draws them on, repeats the following piously-significant prayer :—

"Let my feet be shod, O Lord, with the preparation of the "Gospel of Peace; and protect me under the shadow of thy "wings."

He then slips his feet into the sandals, and, having adjusted them, proceeds to vest himself in the amice, alb, and the rest of the pontifical vestments.

Whenever the bishop celebrates he wears the buskins, except on Good Friday, and at Masses for the Dead.

Plate 35.

BORDERS FOR ALBS

The Sandals.

XXXI.

THE SANDALS.

THE earliest form of Sandal worn by the priesthood generally was probably similar to that still used by many religious orders, *i. e.* of leathern soles, secured on the foot by thongs, or straps, across the instep.

Simultaneously, the episcopal sandals were also made of leather, but of a much superior kind. It was delicately stained or tinted with colour, and ornamented by a perforated pattern, which exhibited itself most effectively over the naked instep.

Of such were the sandals described as found in the grave of St. Cuthbert, buried A.D. 687.

In the twelfth century, the bishop's sandals were no longer made solely of the *windowed* leather, as it was termed, but were sometimes beautifully embroidered on the richest silks, and made costly, as other pontifical appointments, with gold, silver, and pearls.

Dr. Rock concludes that the "corium fenestratum," or open-worked "leather sandal, fell into disuse about the fourteenth "century, in England, when it was left in possession of the "laity."

From the latter part of the eleventh century to the above-named period the episcopal sandals were made of nearly every colour, but principally of scarlet; and hence, as the writer just quoted asserts (from the authority of Sicard), arose the name of *sandal*, from the red dye with which the leather was coloured.

Church Vestments.

About the beginning of the twelfth century, it would appear that the use of various-coloured sandals, to any but the higher order of the clergy, was prohibited, and *black* only was recommended to be worn by the priesthood as most suitable to their degree. This was particularly laid down by the Council of Exeter, A.D. 1287, and still more strictly enjoined in the Council of London, A.D. 1342.

The earliest example we have met with of the bishop's ornamental sandal is that presented on the figures of the bishops of Ravenna, Plate 5.

At no period could the episcopal shoe have been much richer in decoration than these mosaics show.

Next, in chronological order, is the fine old sandal we have copied from the "Vetus Liturgia Alemannica" of Gerbert, who supposes it to have belonged to St. Egino, Bishop of Verona, who died A.D. 802. This is exhibited on Plate 36, fig. 7.

In the above work a separate illustration is given of each shoe. The writer met with them at Reichenau, near Constance, and describes them as of leather, which appears once to have been stained purple, figured upon with needlework. Fig. 8, Plate 36, is an illustration of the shoe of an archbishop, sculptured on Chartres Cathedral early in the twelfth century. The mitre exhibited, fig. 6, on the same Plate, is also taken from this effigy, which is engraved in Shaw's " Dresses and Decorations of the " Middle Ages."

The sandals of Bishop Giffard, in which he was buried in Worcester Cathedral, A.D. 1301, are shown on the above Plate, fig. 9. It is curious to note, notwithstanding that a period of six centuries may have rolled between the one and the other, how nearly these shoes resemble, in shape and workmanship, the sandals of the right-hand figure on Plate 5.

The Sandals.

Like the rest of his dress, the sandals of Thomas De la Mare, Plate 11, are beautiful examples of their kind, and prove to us, more and more, how, in the fourteenth century, propriety in ornament was clearly the leading principle of its beauty. The design upon these shoes is perfect, and we are willing to suppose that full justice was rendered to it in work and materials.

Of a very different style, though still handsome, is the shoe of Bishop Waneflete, of the latter part of the fifteenth century, fig. 10, Plate 36.

The original is kept at St. Mary Magdalen College, Oxford. Our copy is from the excellent drawing of it published in the "Church of our Fathers," from which we have also extracted its description:—

" It is of crimson velvet, of a rich deep pile, and wrought with
" flowers in gold, and with leaves like ivy, of silk, half yellow,
" half green; the little dots of gold, with which the velvet is
" thickly sprinkled, are found very often on English vestments
" of the latter part of the fifteenth century.

" It is lined with very thin white kid."

It was this same Bishop Waneflete who drew up statutes for his college at Oxford, wherein he imposed the greatest strictures upon the fellows and scholars of the University in regard to their dress; forbidding them to wear " high-lows, or red, or peaked " boots," or garments of any description which could not be held " suitable and agreeable to the priestly state."

The episcopal sandals, or shoes, of the present day, which the bishop always wears when he says Mass, are usually formed of a rich material called lama,* a fabrication of either gold or silver,

---

* Lama, in the Italian, is explained as "a blade, a thin plate of metal." The woof of the fabric to which this name is given, is partly formed by silver, or gold metal, drawn to

Church Vestments.

woven equally with silk. They are made up with ordinary leather single soles, and are lined with white kid. The depth is that of a tolerably high shoe, the back quarters lapping over the front, where they are brought together, and tied with a bow of ribbon on the instep.

The bishop's sandals are mostly embroidered with gold, in various designs, which, like those for the gloves, must be left to the taste and discretion of the worker. The sandals are always changed, with the other vestments, to the colour of the day. They are worn neither in Masses for the Dead nor on Good Fridays.

the thinnest strips, or threads; while silk constitutes the warp, and embodies the ground colour, of which the metal is the enriching property.

The use of this material is very general in Rome for ecclesiastical purposes. Orphreys to velvet, or silk copes, are often made of it, and even without the addition of needlework, have a very beautiful effect.

One who has lately returned from Rome, and who is not only interested, but learned, in our subject, writes us as follows, in regard to the use of lama, in the Church of the Holy See :—

"The Pope himself wears nothing richer than this, for I believe it impossible to conceive "any material more pure-looking, more brilliant, and yet more *unworldly*-like, than the "silver lama, when made, into vestments. On Easter Sunday his Holiness is arrayed in "silver lama enriched with gold embroidery, with no colour added, except that seen in the "jewels, and the small amount contributed by the fanon. Indeed, all the sacerdotal vest-"ments, on the grand Paschal celebration at St. Peter's, are of silver lama, and wonderfully "is its purity of effect heightened by the scarlet and violet of the cardinals' and bishops' "robes."

The writer of the above was good enough to procure, for our information, patterns of lama from one of its best makers in Rome—Angelo Bianchi, Via della Minerva, 82, 83.

We find that gold, silver, red, green, violet, and black, average 28*s*. per yard in Italy; and may be imported here at less than 40*s*. per yard, after carriage and duty are paid.

A lama vestment, we are told, of any colour, richly embroidered in gold and silks, may be obtained from Bianchi for 22*l*.

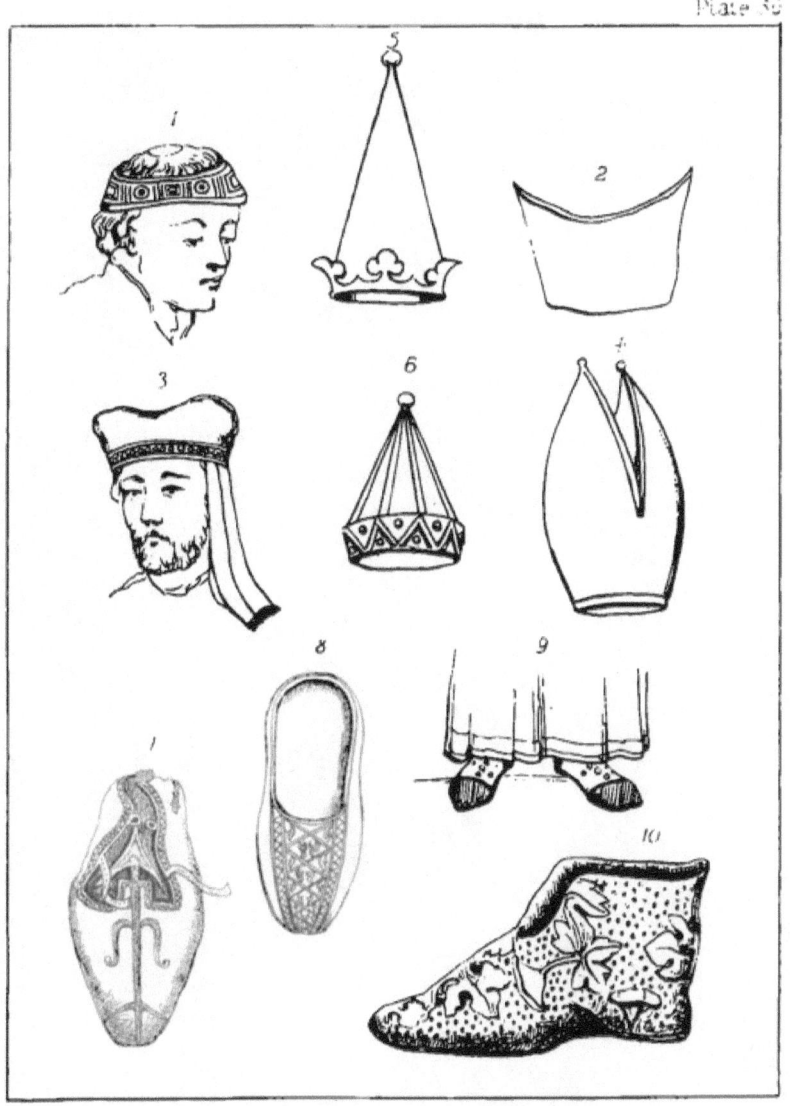

THE MITRE AND SANDALS

XXXII.

THE GLOVES.

THE bishop's gloves, known in old ecclesiastical records under the names of *manicæ* and *chirothecæ*, have probably been in use from a period as distant as the seventh century, if not from an earlier date.

We find the term *manicæ* (sleeves) to be not wholly misapplied to these sacerdotal appurtenances in their ancient form, since they were made to draw up over the hand, considerably above the wrist, where in after ages they terminated, at the under side of the arm, in a gracefully-turned point, from the extremity of which hung a tassel.

Gloves are distinctly named in the old Salisbury Pontifical, where a beautiful prayer is framed, to be said by the bishop elect as he draws them on. In olden times, it is clear that other orders of the clergy, as well as the bishop, wore gloves at the Divine services. In some parts of France, especially, such was the habit; for De Vert remarks upon the priors of Clugni officiating in gloves, and upon cantors at Tours, and some other places, holding their staves with gloved hands. The same writer also mentions that at Angers, and many such churches, the reliquary bearers performed their functions in gloves. This custom, against which no injunction exists, may be very properly followed, at the present day, by canopy, banner, and candle-bearers, in the sacred offices of the Church.

Church Vestments.

The gloves of the minor orders of the clergy were, we may justly presume, without any decoration of importance, and were in every other respect inferior to those of the prelate, which, as far as we can trace, were, from the time of St. Osmund, always ornamented, and frequently richly embroidered, and studded with gold and gems.

The inventory of Old St. Paul's, A.D. 1295, helps us to a description of episcopal gloves treasured there at that period:—

"A mitre, seeded with pearls all over, the gift of Bishop "Richard," comes first; and then "two gloves of the like work-"manship, the gift of the same, in which many stones are "wanting. Also two pair of gloves, ornamented with silver "plates gilt, and set with stones."

Pugin, in giving the above extract, couples with it the following, from the inventory of Canterbury Cathedral, published in Dart's History:—

"Cirotecæ. R. de Winchelese cum perlis et gemmis in plata "quadrata. Item, par unum cum tasselis * argenteis et parvis "lapidibus. Item, quatuor paria, cum tasselis argenteis. Item, "par unum de lino, cum tasselis et perlis."

In the first days of their adoption the bishop's gloves are supposed to have been always white, and of linen. Subsequently, they were made of silk, and of various colours, to accord with the vestments of the day;† but of the precise period when the use of any but white were sanctioned we are uncertain. Some

---

* These "tasselli" are not to be read as the ornaments called *tassels* of our day, but as those little plates of precious metal sewn down upon the material, and described as enriching much of the old vestment work. On the figure of Archbishop Chicheley, in Canterbury Cathedral, the gloves are embellished with silver "tasselli."

† Red would seem to have been the prevailing colour of the episcopal gloves, judging from those figured upon ancient monuments.

The Gloves.

writers, Durandus among the rest, assert that in the thirteenth century the prelate's gloves were still white.

Those in which Pope Boniface the Eighth was buried in the fourteenth century were of white silk, richly figured with embroidery and fine pearls; while the glove of William of Wykeham, preserved at New College, Oxford, which must have been made either late in the fourteenth, or very early in the fifteenth century, is of purple silk, ornamented with gold.

On the figure of Thomas de la Mare, Plate 11, the gloves show a lozenge-shaped device on the back; this was, doubtless, some gem, or other ornament of a costly character, such as the munificent abbot, with his true taste for the beautiful in sacerdotal dress, would have judged in harmony with the rest of those gracefully-adorned vestments.

The gloves of the Roman Catholic bishop are now always made of woven silk, embellished with gold embroidery, and are worn to correspond in colour with the vestments of the day. On Good Fridays, and Masses for the Dead, the bishop wears no gloves.

The most correct form of glove made for the episcopal use is that with a top, widened from the wrist, as a gauntlet, and terminating in two points at the under side of the arm. Around this cuff, or gauntlet-shaped piece, a narrow border of gold bullion embroidery is usually worked, besides the decoration on the back of the hand, for which any uniform design of a strictly ecclesiastical character is correct.

A cross within a circle; the sacred monogram, inclosed by a floriated quatrefoil; or a conventional rose, enriched by seed-pearls, or by small well-set jewels, may be esteemed equally appropriate for the adornment of the bishop's gloves.

As the difficulty of embroidering with nicety on a made-up

glove, particularly on one of woven silk, is great, we strongly urge the worker to execute the principal part of the design, viz., that which covers the back of the hand, on fine linen, and transfer it afterwards. The process of working the narrow border actually upon the gauntlet, which is the only proper way, will be found very easy.

XXXIII.

THE PALLIUM.

THE archbishop's Pallium, incontrovertibly said to be the legitimate descendant of the Roman toga, is worn as the symbol of jurisdiction.

In the time of St. Gregory the Great, the pall, or pallium, seems to have been a long strip of material, woven of plain white lamb's wool, and worn about the figure in such a way that it crossed over the left shoulder, from which the ends were allowed to fall, before and behind. This is exhibited, in our earliest example of the pall, on the Bishops of Ravenna, Plate 5.

It does not appear that the above manner of wearing the pallium was changed until the beginning of the ninth century, when we find it shifted round, so that its ends, though still drooping before and behind, hung down the centre of the figure, instead of falling from the left shoulder, as heretofore.

The next modification was, as hitherto, simply in the *arrangement* of the pallium. It was fixed to the breast and back of the wearer, and at the left shoulder, where, in crossing, the material was necessarily doubled, by three gold pins.

It then took its first, really, *altered*, and what we may call its final, form; for, excepting its curtailment in length, the pall is the same shape now as it was in the thirteenth century. It was woven with a circular band to embrace the shoulders, and with

Church Vestments

long ends hanging straight down, back and front of the figure, as see St. Peter, Plate 8, and archbishop, on Plate 30.

For centuries the pallium was figured only with a purple, or sometimes a red, cross at each end. Then four crosses were worked about it; and, finally, six, worked in black, were figured over it: its ends, too, were shortened, and it became as it remains, and as we present it on Plate 37, sketched as it is worn by the Pope over his fanon.

The pallium has always been made in Rome, whither every archbishop must go to receive it direct from the Holy See. He wears it always when he sings the solemn High Mass in his own diocese, but not out of it; and it is the only one of his pontificals which he may not lend to a brother primate.

The Pope wears the pallium when, and wherever, he says Mass. The pallium is still made only of pure white wool, and fastened by the three gold pins.

The ceremony of blessing the lambs, of whose wool the pallium is formed, is a very interesting one.

We describe it from Dr. Rock's already well-told account of it:—

"Every year, on the morning of St. Agnes's Feast, the 21st "of January, a horse, bearing slung over his back two baskets, "each of which holds a lamb of the fairest and the whitest, is to "be seen walking into Rome, from the country, towards the "Pope's palace, before which it awaits till the Pontiff comes to a "window, thrown wide open, and, standing there, makes the sign "of the cross upon the bleating burden below him.

"Borne thence to the fine old basilican church of St. Agnes, "out of the walls, where solemn High Mass is to be sung, these "lambs, decked with ribbons and flowers, are taken to the altar, "and kept at its foot while the Holy Sacrifice is offered up.

The Pallium.

"Formerly, at the Agnus Dei, but now after Divine service is ended, the celebrating priest goes through the ceremony of blessing these little animals.

"They are then given over to the canons of the Pope's Cathedral (St. John Lateran's), and the chapter of that church sends them to the Pontiff himself, who orders them to be conveyed unto the dean of the apostolic sub-deacons, by whom they are entrusted to the care of some nunnery, where they are kept and fed. In due time these lambs are shorn, and their fleeces, along with which is put, if need be, other fine wool, are spun and woven by the nuns into palls, against the festival of SS. Peter and Paul."

The old pallium is still commemorated on the arms of the see of Canterbury.

XXXIV.

THE FANON.

THE *Fanon* is the "*orale*" of ancient Catholic days. It typifies the ephod of the high priest of the Jewish Law, and therefore appertains only to the vesture of the Sovereign Pontiff.

When the Pope solemnly pontificates, he wears the fanon above his chasuble; but before he assumes that garment, the fanon is placed upon his head as a hood; then, when the sacrificial vestment is arranged about his body, the fanon is turned down, and smoothly laid over his neck and shoulders, to be surmounted by the pallium, as shown, Plate 37.

The fanon is made of a material, in texture, as light as gauze, and is figured with gold, blue, and red, in stripes.

THE FANON, AND PALLIUM

XXXV.

THE CASSOCK.

TO describe the form and make of this garment lies not within our province, as it exclusively belongs to that of the clerical tailor.

All orders of the clergy wear the cassock made after the same model. The soutane, or cassock, of the Pope is always *white*, that of cardinals scarlet, and of bishops and prelates purple.

Priests and assistants at the Divine services wear alike the black cassock. An exception to this rule is, however, sometimes made, such as when at a Pontifical High Mass, as shown in our Frontispiece, the acolytes are permitted to use the bishop's colour, purple, for their cassocks.

XXXVI.

THE BIRETTA.

THE Biretta, anciently worn by canons in choir, is especially the cap of the duly-ordained priest.

When vested for the holy sacrifice of the Mass, the priest, deacon, and sub-deacon proceed from the sacristy to the sanctuary wearing their birettas, which, as they approach the altar, are removed and placed on the sedilia at the south side of the chancel. When the Gloria is about to be sung by the choir, the priests seat themselves, and resume their caps.

All through the Divine service the priests divest themselves of the biretta before advancing to the altar, and wear it whenever they are seated. At every part of the Liturgy, or during the sermon, where the Holy Name is repeated, or the Incarnation alluded to, the biretta is reverentially raised both by priest and preacher.

XXXVII.

THE ROMAN COLLAR.

THE priest's Roman Collar, as it is called, is a conventional appurtenance of recent date, adopted by the clergy to simulate the turn-down shirt-collar of ordinary dress.

It is well known that all priests, up to the latter half of the sixteenth century, went with the neck and throat perfectly bare, and that the collar has even as little claim to antiquity as the Lutheran ruff, or the Geneva black gown; and is altogether ignored by most of the older religious orders.

Still, the Roman collar is anything but an unseemly addition to the cassock, or to the clerical coat, and, if it continue to be worn of the present regulation size and shape, may yet hold its own against all secular fashions, as a distinguishing mark of a clergyman's attire.

The collar worn by priests generally is made of a perfectly straight piece of fine linen, or lawn. It is bordered on the turn-over side, and along its short ends, by a neatly-stitched hem of half an inch. Opened out, when made, it is $2\frac{3}{4}$ inches wide; the turn-down should not be more than $1\frac{1}{2}$ inch deep.

The length of the collar is, of course, controlled by the size of the wearer's throat. The average measure is from $15\frac{1}{2}$ to 16 inches.

The Roman collar worn by a bishop is violet, that of a cardinal is scarlet.

Church Vestments.

XXXVIII.

PROPER COLOURS FOR THE SACRED VESTMENTS.

ACCORDING to the Roman Rubric, only *five* positive colours are allotted to the Church for the sacred vestments, viz., white, red, green, violet, and black.

Each of these is used as under:—

1. White, emblematical of purity, on all feasts of our Lord but those of His Passion; on festivals of the Blessed Virgin; of the saints, not martyrs; and, according to the strict Roman rite, on festivals of the blessed Sacrament.

2. Red, on the feasts of Pentecost, and the apostles and martyrs; as symbolical of the descent of the Holy Ghost, in the form of fiery tongues; and of the shedding of the blood of the Redeemer and His faithful followers.

3. Green, on every Sunday upon which a festival does not fall, excepting those in Advent and Lent, and those which, coming within the octave of a festival, must follow its rule, and assume its colour.

4. Violet, the penitential colour, and therefore worn in Advent and Lent, on the Rogation-days, Ember-days, and on all Vigils.

5. Black, only on Good Friday, and in Masses for the Dead.

Besides these, cloth of gold must be mentioned, as allowed to take the place of any colour, except black and violet.

Gold, too, may be used to any extent in the way of ornament, on any coloured vestment but black, upon which only silver or

Proper Colours for the Sacred Vestments.

white silk embroideries may be figured. It is also ordered that each colour should be so represented, that its use may distinctly mark the particular day upon which the Church requires it to be worn. It is forbidden to mingle white, red, and green indefinitely in one vestment, so that it may be used indiscriminately on any day for which either of these colours is ordered.

According to the old Sarum rite, not only were sky-blue and yellow recognised colours for the sacred vestments, but *red* was used in Lent, and on Good Friday.

From Dugdale alone we get ample proof of the observation of this rite. He enumerates blue vestments of every degree as belonging to St. Frideswide's Monastery—now Christ Church, Oxford,—Peterborough, and Winchester.

In the vestiary inventory of St. Frideswide's we light upon "copes of blew silk with flower-de-luces, roses, and crowns of "gold, and a hole sute to the same. A cope of blew velvett "with braunches of gold, and a sute to the same;" and even "three albes, and three amesses of blew cloth baundekin."

A large space in the Peterborough list is taken up by blue vestments. One of its prominent items is of "forty blew albes "of divers sorts."

Winchester Monastery is set down for "forty-two copys of "tisshue, one half of them blue, the other of red;" and "nine- "and-twenty copys of blue silk, woven with rays of gold."

In our observation of the sub-deacon's vestment, page 84, we have said that, formerly, celestial blue was the colour of the dalmatic and tunicle of the bishop. That such blue sacred garments as are enumerated in the above inventories were worn in our English churches on festivals of the blessed Virgin, as white has always been, we are unable to prove satisfactorily.

Dr. Rock remarks that he saw sky-blue used in Spain, and in

Church Vestments.

Naples, at the services of our Lady. He also directs us to the Ordo Romanus XV., drawn up by Peter Amelio, who flourished A.D. 1393, to find that light blue was once employed at Rome, which now excludes it altogether from the sanctuary, as a substitute for black or purple.

Red is continually occurring in the old lists of sacerdotal possessions as the colour, enjoined by the Sarum rite, for Lent and Good Friday. The first item in Dugdale's account of the albs found at Peterborough in 1539 is—

"Red albs for *Passion-week*, twenty-seven."

We have written evidence, too, from many sources, of the use of *yellow* vestments, here as well as abroad, in Lent. This is especially confirmed to us in the following from the inventory of Lincoln Cathedral. Moreover, the item appears under the heading of "*black* vestments :"—

"Chesable of yellow silk, small orphrey, crucifix of gold in "red on the back, 2 tunacles, 3 albs, and the whole apparel, with "2 copes of the same suit and colour for *Lent*."

Violet, or purple, was certainly a less favoured colour for penitential seasons in the Church of the mediæval period than it is now; for, throughout all our late research in behalf of this work, we have found but a meagre mention of purple in any record.

Even in the richly-stocked wardrobe of Lincoln the paucity of purple vestments is remarkable, *blue*, in comparison, being truly abundant.

Embroidery Stitches.

XXXIX.

EMBROIDERY STITCHES OF THE ANGLO-SAXON AND EARLY MEDIÆVAL PERIODS.

THE more ancient the needlework, the more remarkable do we find it for beauty of effect, gained by simple means. The designs exhibited on the oldest relics of embroidered vestments are of the plainest, although frequently of the most symbolic, character; and in their execution by the needle, not a stitch has been used which, if drawn away, would not leave the pattern incomplete.

One great feature of the Anglo-Saxon work was its lightness. The gold and silks were made to *trace* the pattern, as it were, on the surface of the main fabric of the article ornamented.

It is easy to account, in some degree, for this peculiarity, when we reflect that in those early days such rich materials were costly beyond our conception now, and were, doubtless, economized, and, at the same time, made the most of upon these sacred garments, the general decoration of which was held so essential.

There is a growing taste for the revival of this graceful description of sacred embroidery. Most of our leading architects are adopting the ancient style of ornament in church decoration, and, where they are consulted in the matter of vestments, encourage, and very properly, a preference for works of the needle which are in character with the building wherein they are to be used.

Church Vestments.

In "Church Embroidery," we limited our practical illustrations of stitches to those principally of the mediæval period: we here give twelve examples, the first *eight* of which may be accepted as true types of the sacred needlework of the very earliest Christian times. Indeed, we are not sure whether, like the "gammadion," this method of embroidering was not in vogue ages before the year of our Lord; for much of the Eastern work, at this very day, is remarkable for the greater part of its rich materials being kept upon the surface of the velvet, silk, or cloth it is used to ornament. This is especially the case with the gold thread, and twist, wrought upon those tastefully decorated garments from India and Algeria, sometimes seen for sale in this country.

In the following eight patterns, silks of any rich colours, with gold twist, and thread, are to be employed where these different materials are indicated in the engraving.

The first, and unexceptionably the most ancient of these designs worked upon, what we may call, the outline principle, is the "gammadion," explained page 138. This forms the pattern

No. 1.

on the stole, Plate 34. It may be worked as a border to a Y cross, on the chasuble, and also for the edge of the garment.

Embroidery Stitches.

For the "Mitra auriphrygiata" no device could be more suitable, upon the bands or orphreys, than the "gammadion."

The next imitation of an Anglo-Saxon border tells its own age by its quaint simplicity. It will be seen to resemble the figuring upon the head-band of St. Benedict, Plate 36, and originated, probably, in the "gammadion," to which it certainly shows an affinity.

No. 2.

No. 3 is an exceedingly pretty pattern, in rich colours and gold; it is less bold or effective than some others, but, notwithstanding, is a good specimen of the more elaborated needlework of an early date.

No. 3.

No. 4 may either be worked upon an embroidered silk ground, as represented here, or it may be executed only in outline. It is a good pattern for the border of a Bendiction burse, a chalice veil, a gremiale, or any sacred article of moderate dimensions. Gold beads have been used here with great advantage.

Church Vestments.

No. 4.

One of our most favourite outline designs is No. 5; expressive, and easy of accomplishment. It will be recognized as forming the circular pattern on the hood with crowns, Plate 25. As a border on each side of a plain velvet, or a cloth of gold, orphrey, for the cope of the above hood, this would be perfect. On any fabric, or upon any colour, it will stand out, when worked, with good effect. Berlin silk, gold passing, twist, and gold beads, are all the materials required for its production.

No. 5.

The above is the kind of border suggested for the offertory veil, page 114.

No. 6 is another suitable border for the decoration of the garment last named. We have used gold beads very profusely

Embroidery Stitches.

in some of these patterns, and are well satisfied with the result. Beads are so easily laid in their places upon the work, and ensure repeated *regularity*, in a formal pattern where round dots are indicated. Moreover, their enriching properties are invaluable, when brought to bear with coloured silks.

No. 6.

The unpretending little border illustrated in No. 7 is also made the circular pattern surrounding the figure of the Agnus Dei on a hood, shown Plate 25.

As an embroidered edging to the orphrey of a cope, or for the decoration of the offertory veil, this design is as eligible as that of No. 5.

No. 7.

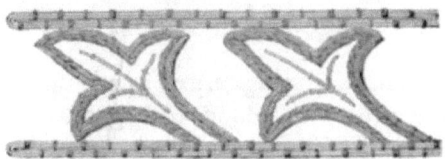

Our engraver has so well represented the different materials we have used in the development of these patterns, that we

Church Vestments.

believe it scarcely necessary to say that only one kind of rich twist silk, "passing," and sewings, have been employed for this.

Our last pattern for silk and gold is copied from a missal of the thirteenth century, and is gorgeous enough in colour and general effect, to make us wish that it had been possible to present it to every eye, as we see it at this moment. Indeed, we might say this of all these particular designs worked in outline; they can never be fully appreciated until they are set forth in colours and gold. To have illustrated them in this manner here would have made our book too costly for its specific purpose; we can, therefore, only urge our readers to work them, that they may find themselves fascinated, as we are, by the truly grand effects which can be produced in a short space of time by moderate patience, and a fair amount of skill.

No. 8.

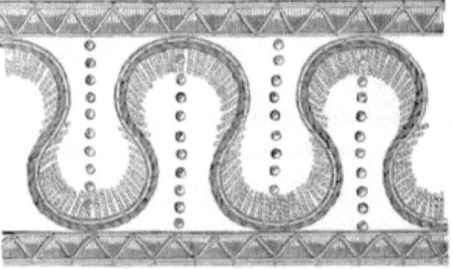

The following four engravings are of patterns in "passing," as it is used to enrich the backgrounds to figures, and other objects, on the vestment work of mediæval times.

Our space restricting us to this number, only, of illustrations, we select such as will serve for examples of the principle upon which these stitch patterns on gold are made, and may be multi-

Embroidery Stitches.

plied. In "Church Embroidery" we gave thirteen such elementary specimens, to which these may be considered a supplement.

It is impossible to show, upon paper, the numberless ways in which the ancient workers, particularly of the fifteenth and sixteenth centuries, raised their embroidery, by string and other means.

Many of the German vestments in the South Kensington Museum exhibit this style to an exaggerated extent; for, rich as some portions of a design may be made in relief, other parts become coarse and common by the like treatment; and this is to be observed on some of the garments referred to. As, for example, on a chasuble of Cologne work, of the fifteenth century, where the subject is the Crucifixion, the features of the Saviour are rendered most painfully *material* by the height to which they are raised beneath the flesh-coloured silks. So with those of the Blessed Virgin, figured upon this garment; anything more stolid and matter-of-fact than her face cannot be conceived, owing to the efforts of the worker to put them in strong relief, by mechanical means. This is only one of several subjects in the same collection, which we could point to, as likely to mislead the modern Church-needlewoman in her ambition to copy effective ancient embroidery.

The work of the thirteenth and fourteenth centuries was essentially refined in every phase. On the wonderful Abergavenny chasuble, Plate 12, the whole of that beautiful background, to the Crucifixion, is laid without a particle of string. Its raised effect is brought about by an ingenious manner of working the stitches, in "wavy couching," into a pattern, as they regulate the gold thread on the linen foundation.

However, there are certain classes of ecclesiastical design, and particular forms, where stitch patterns in relief are not only admissible, but necessary to the perfection of richness. Of such are some backgrounds, borderings, and canopies to figures; though the figures themselves, and, above all, their features, should be put in relief, only, by *flat shading*.

No. 9 is a ground pattern of the fifteenth century, but not a raised one. It may be seen on a chasuble of German work, at South Kensington, where the wheels are of gold passing, stitched with crimson, on an embroidered ground of crimson floss. It is very rich, and costly looking.

No. 9. No. 10.

We publish No. 10, not that it is wonderful, but because it is pretty and chaste, and so very appropriate, as we have seen it used in fifteenth-century embroidery, for a drapery of our Lady.

It is of gold "passing," couched all over, in this little diamond pattern, with celestial blue. The cloak of the same figure is of green silk, worked in long-stitch, with lines of "passing" laid against the dark shade, to mark the folds. The lining of this garment is blue floss, of the same shade as the couching stitches.

Embroidery Stitches.

No. 11 is one of the raised stitches which we have remarked as popular with the needleworkers of the fifteenth and sixteenth centuries.

We have done our best to show the manner of laying the string, which is the principle itself, for the accomplishment of such a pattern.

No. 12 is given to exemplify the ease with which raised patterns may be varied, only by laying the string in different formal ways.

This example has been copied from one, among many of the back-grounds to large subjects, with which the relics of sacred needlework, of the later Mediæval period, have made us so familiar.

No. 11.

No. 12.

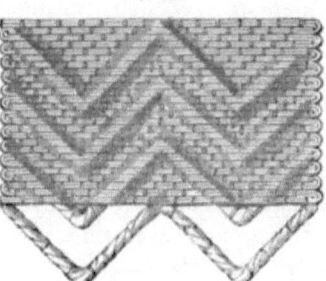

Church Vestments.

XL.

THE VESTMENT-MAKER'S CHARGE TO THE SACRISTAN.

WHERE the province of the vestment-maker ends, there does that of the sacristan begin.

We have just reached the prescribed limit of our subject, and, before leaving it, would say a few words respecting the good keeping of those sacred robes, for the seemly decoration of which we have lovingly laboured through so many pages.

As a hint to sacristans generally, we would first remark that upon their care does the preservation of the contents of the sacerdotal wardrobe mainly depend.

Tables free from dust and grease, so that they may be touched or anything laid upon them without fear of soil, and a constant adherence to the old maxim " of a place for every-" thing, and everything in its place," are conditions which every wardrobe-keeper should feel bound to fulfil, as essential to the conscientious discharge of the general duties of his post.

Besides these, a deliberate examination of each robe as, after its use, it is given to his charge, to remove any mark, or spot of wax which it may have received; gentle brushing, even folding, and smooth laying in its assigned place, are all simple acts of care, to be observed as imperative; for the neglect of any one of them might cause irreparable injury to some beautiful object

The Vestment-maker's Charge to the Sacristan.

of intrinsic value to the church, which the best intentions, with the most liberal means, could never again replace.

Nor should the sacristan be interfered with, or called aside when he is engaged in putting away the priests' robes. This sometimes happens, and the vestments are hastily laid in the drawers, and, maybe, forgotten till they are next required, when they are produced in a condition which would be anything but seemly, even for articles of ordinary apparel. Indeed, a well-bred man would consider his valet unfit for his situation, were he to present him with a creased garment, or a coat unbrushed, since it was last worn. What then should not be expected from a sacred wardrobe keeper?

A well-constructed vestiary will be fitted with presses filled with drawers, and sliding doors beyond, for the exclusion of air, as well as dust. The drawers should be wide, that the vestments may be saved from much folding, and shallow, that they may be numerous; for it is a much better plan to keep each set of vestments in a separate drawer, if possible, than to fill up a deep space by laying many robes one over the other, to be injured either by their own weight, or by being lifted up, and turned over, to extract from the heap any particular set.

The priests' robes of linen, and the acolytes and choristers' surplices, should be kept in separate drawers, and most carefully folded every time they are laid by.

The sacred linen of the altar must also be kept apart from the vestments, before it has been once used. Afterwards, the priest who has used it will order its destination.

Velvet vestments require great care in putting away. They should be folded, with pads of wadding between to obviate creasing, across, not lengthwise; and the less they are folded the better.

Church Vestments.

The protection of bullion embroidery and cloth of gold from damp and bad air is another important duty of the sacristan. The drawers wherein vestments enriched by the precious metals are kept should be lined with thick flannel—not green baize, for the green dye is fugitive, and destructive to gold and silver. Covers of unbleached calico, which have been steeped in saffron water, should also be provided to fold about the garments when they are laid by; and even layers of the same saffron-dyed calico, placed over the gold embroidery itself, will protect it from the influence of a pernicious atmosphere better than anything else.

The most striking example of the careful preservation of modern gold work is instanced in a costly set of crimson velvet vestments, presented in the year 1853, by Sir George Bowyer, to St. George's Cathedral, Southwark.

Originally intended for an Italian church, dedicated to St. Peter, they are of the Roman shape, and were worked and made under our direction, from the designs of Mr. T. J. Burton.

Their embellishment consists of rich gold embroidery, and orphreys of lace, woven, for this express gift, with the keys and sword in bright gold, upon a green ground, figured here and there with crimson.

That the metal used in the manufacture of the lace was pure as it could be, time has, in some degree, shown, for it is still brilliant, as when it left the weaver's hands. The bullion embroidery, too, on the chasuble, offertory veil, stoles, and the rest, we find scarcely dimmed; neither is the gold thread, so profusely used in the cords and tassels of the dalmatics, and veil, tarnished.

This is much to be able to say, after a test of fifteen years' constant wear, of the manufactured gold of modern days. We

The Vestment-maker's Charge to the Sacristan.

give all due credit to the excellent quality of the metal, but find that we have much praise left in reserve for the memory of the late excellent sacristan, to whose great, not to say reverential, care the preservation of these beautiful objects has, doubtless, been in a great part owing.

It is true that every church is not favoured with such a vestiary as St. George's, which, as A. W. Pugin planned it, may be considered nearly perfect. But space, and appointed drawers, fitted to exclude air and dust, and to receive every article of the sacerdotal dress, without much folding, are not all-sufficient. The sacristan should not only be calculated to feel a greater respect for the robes of the holy altar than for those, however costly, which belong to secular clothing, but he should also have some degree of knowledge of the different materials which, by virtue of his office, he has to handle.

Twenty years ago, such a man might have been difficult to find, to occupy this post, in the Church of England; for we believe that no power on earth could have converted the stereotyped parish clerk of half a century back into the duly qualified verger, or sacristan.

Happily, however, this is not now the condition of such things, in any church where its rites are solemnly observed; and we can suppose, that in every band of choristers, or acolytes, there is a youth, of good principles and right feeling, ready to be selected for initiation, and instruction, in the duties of a sacristan.

Apart from the honour of such an appointment, it is worthy of being made sufficiently lucrative to meet the necessary wants of one who is respectable enough to make it his vocation, and upon whose care so much that is of true value to the dignity of the Christian Ritual depends. In some churches there

Church Vestments.

are members of the clergy, who not only interest themselves, but delight, æsthetically, in the real business of the sacred wardrobe.

Such as these, we say it deferentially, are the best fitted to impart knowledge on the subject, with as much as possible of their taste, to all aspiring to the sacristan's office.

Description of Frontispiece.

DESCRIPTION OF FRONTISPIECE.

THE subject of our frontispiece was suggested through our desire to show as many of the sacred robes as possible in actual use.

We need scarcely explain that the bishop is the celebrant, on this occasion; and that the figure by his side, robed in a cope, is his assistant at the Mass, and therefore, for the time being, highest in degree, next to the prelate himself, of the clergy at the altar.

The deacon is being incensed by the acolyte. The sub-deacon stands at the foot of the altar, shrouding the paten with the offertory veil.

The surpliced figure next to the sub-deacon is the master of the ceremonies, whose functions are as important as they are held sacred, at every solemn High Mass, in the Catholic Church.

The acolytes bearing the mitre and staff of the bishop, wear a scarf, usually of white crape, around their necks, for the purpose of muffling their hands, to hold the episcopal insignia.

The altar itself has been adapted to our views, from one of many beautiful designs of the kind, generously placed at our

Church Vestments.

disposal, by Messrs. Mayer, of Holles Street, Cavendish Square, and of Munich.

The reputation of this house for sacred works of art, in the precious metals and other materials, is already great; it is likely to become, as it deserves, world-wide.

Index.

Abergavenny, Description of Ancient Vestments found at, 18, 183.
Agnus Dei, Description of, on Chasuble, 60.
Aix-la-Chapelle, Ancient Chasuble at, 46.
Alb, The, 31.
———, Ancient Example of, at South Kensington, 37.
———, Apparels of, 34.
———, Correct Dimensions of, 38.
———, Empress Eugénie, to Pope Pius the Ninth, presented by, 36.
———, First decoration of, 33.
———, The Sacrificial Ministering Robe, 122.
———, Worn over the Rochet, 145.
Albs, Coloured, 31.
———, Costly Gifts of, 34, 36.
———, Worn by Children, 146.
Almucia, The. See Amys, 132.
Altar, The, Description of, on Frontispiece, 191.
———, Sacred Linen of, 127, 187.
Amice, The, 26.
———, Adorned with precious stones, 102.
———, Apparels of, 28.
———, Description of Ancient Example of, at South Kensington, 29.
Amys, The Furred, 132.
Ancient Vestments, Description of, at the Great Exhibition, 1862, 15.
———, Examples of, at South Kensington, 21, 183.

Index.

Anglo-Saxon Bishop, Head-linen of the, 136.
———————, Mitre of the, 135.
———————, Subcingulum of the, 149.
Anglo-Saxon Clergy, Chasuble worn by the, 48.
———————, Cope of the, 104.
———————, Offertory Veil of the, 114.
———————, "Roc" or Tunicle of the, 83.
———————, Surplice originated by the, 121.
Anglo-Saxon "Flower," The, on the Chasuble, 57.
Anglo-Saxon Stitches, 177.
Annunciation, The, Chasuble designed for, Description of, 67.
Arnulph, Prior of Rochester, Gift of, of Rich Vestment, and Cope with Silver Bells, 102.

Bath Abbey, Gifts of Vestments to, 12.
"Bawdkin," 70.
Beaufort, Cardinal, Rich Gift of, to Winchester, 13.
Benedict the Twelfth, Constitution of, on the Surplice, 122.
Benediction Burse, The, 120.
Benediction Veil, The, 113.
Biretta, The, 172.
Blue, Celestial, Used in the Sacred Vestments, 84, 175.
———, Light, anciently substituted for black or purple, 176.
Bobbin-cord, for Chequer-work on Surplice, 124.
Bristol-board, for Burse, 119.
Brocaded Silks, Ancient, 70.
Burse, The Sacrificial, 118.
Buskins, The, 156.
———————, of Bishop Waneflete, 157.
Byzantine Robe, The, of Our Lord, 53.

Calabrian Fur. See Amys, 132.
Calico, Unbleached, 74.
Cambric Shirt, Prince Arthur's, 35.
Campanula. See Note, 91.
Canon's Cope, The, 131.
Canopy and Candle-bearers, Gloves recommended for, 163.

Index.

Canterbury Cathedral, Extract from Inventory of, 164.
————————, Gloves on Figure of Archbishop in, 164.
Canterbury, See of, Pallium in Arms of the, 169.
Canute, King, Gifts of, to Croyland Abbey, 9.
Cappa Magna, The, 153.
Carew Castle, Ancient Figure from, 50.
Cassock, The, 171.
Cencia de Sabellis, Concerning the Subcingulum, 149.
Chalice-Veil, The, 75, 116.
Chartres Cathedral, Ancient Statue from, 54.
————————, Mitre from Archbishop on, 142.
————————, Shoe from same figure on, 160.
Chasuble, The, 43.
————, Correct Materials for, 68.
————, Diptych, 45.
————, French, 56.
————, Hooded, 45.
————, Italian, 55.
————, St. Augustine's Gift of, to St. Livinus, 47.
————, of St. Thomas of Canterbury, 48.
————, Vesica form of, 47.
Chasubles, Mention of Rich, 9, 10, 11, 13, 14, 15, 17, 18, 19, 21.
Chirothecæ, The. See Gloves, 163.
Clavi, The, 4.
Clavus, the Augustus, 5.
————, The Latus, 5.
Clugni, Priors of, Officiating in Gloves, 163.
Coif, and Coyfe, 28.
Collar, The Roman, 173.
Colobium, The, 78.
Colours, Proper for the Sacred Vestments, 174.
Constantine, Emperor, Robe of Cloth of Gold presented to Macarius by The, 4.
————————, Sacred Ritual in reign of the, 3.
Cope, The, 101.
————, Colours of, for particular days, 109.
————, Cycloid, the right form for, 107.
————, Fringe for, 108.

Index.

Cope, The, Fringe of Bells to, 102.
———, Godfrey de Croyland's gift of, to Gaucelinus, 12.
———, Hood of, 104.
———, How to make up, 108.
———, Later use of, in Durham Cathedral, 103.
———, Orphreys of, 106.
Copes, Mention of particular, 9, 10, 11, 12, 13, 14, 15, 16, 17, 102, 103, 105
Corporal-Case. See Burse, 118.
Corporal-Cloths, 127.
Corporal-Oath, 128.
Cotta, The, 126, 146.
Cotton, "Boar's-Head," for Chequer Work on Surplice, 124.
———, Reel, for Tacking-Stitches, 76.
Credence-Cloth, 130.
Cross, The Latin, 51, 64.
———, The Tau, 50.
———, The Y, 60.
Crosses on Sacred Linen, 128.
Crowns, as Finials to Cross, 66.

Dalmatic, The, 78.
———, Apparels of, 80.
———, General Decoration of, 81.
———, Materials for, 81, 82.
———, Shape of, in France, 81.
Dart's History of Canterbury, Extract from, concerning the Gloves, 164
Diadem, Golden, of St. Benedict, 135.
Diapering, 71.
Dorsal, The, of the Chasuble, 59.

Easter-Day, Ancient Custom of Baptising on the Eve of, 33.
———, Description of the Pope's Robes on, 162.
Eastern Church, Stole of the, 89.
Egelric, Gifts of, to Croyland Abbey, 9.
Embroideries, Ancient, in South Kensington Museum, described, 64.
Embroidery, Bullion, preservation of, 188.
———, Church, General Reference to former Work on, 23.

Index.

Embroidery, Exaggerated, 70.
——————, On Latin Cross, directed, 65.
——————, Stitches, Anglo-Saxon, and Mediæval, 177.
Empress Eugénie, The, Gift of Alb from, to Pius the Ninth, 36.

Fanon, The, 170.
Feather-Work, Copes in, 11.
Figured Silks, 71.
"Flower," The, 57.
Frontispiece, Description of, 191.
"Fylfot," The. See "Gammadion," 139.

"Gammadion," The, Description of, 138.
Garinus, Abbot of St. Alban's, Liberality of, 11.
German Vestments in the South Kensington Museum, 21.
Girdle, The, 40.
Glastonbury Abbey, Rich Vestments of, 8.
Gloves, The, 163.
——————, of Boniface the Eighth, 165.
——————, Correct form of, 165.
——————, Decoration of, 166.
——————, of William of Wykeham, 165.
Gothic Stole, The, 89, 92.
Gremiale, The, 151.

Humerals, The, 59.

Ina, King, Gifts of, to Glastonbury Abbey, 8.
Infulæ of Mitre, 136.

Jaconet Muslin, for inner linings, 74.

Lace, Gold, Bindings, 58.
——————, Orphreys of, 61, 63.
Lace, Silk, for Vestments, 63, 74.
——, Thread, for the Rochet, and Cotta, 146.
Lama, Description of, 161.

Index.

Lambs, Ceremony of blessing the, 168.
Laodiceæ, The Council of, concerning the Stole, 88.
Lappets, The Mitre, 136.
Leofric, Bequest of, of three Copes to his Church of Exeter, 102.
Lichfield, First Archbishop of, 48.
Liege, Church of, Extract from a canon of the, 145.
Lincoln Cathedral, Rich Vestiary possessions of, 14, 20, 32.
Linea Tunica, 144.
Linen, Head, The Bishop's, 136.
Linen Mitre, 143.
Linen, Sacred, of the Altar, 127.
Linings, Calico, 75.
————, Inner, 74.
————, Linen, 115, 117.
————, Silk, 75.
————, Woollen, 73.

Macarius, Bishop of Jerusalem, Gift of Constantine to, 4.
Manicæ. See Gloves, 163.
Maniple, The, 93.
————, Origin of, 93.
————, Pugin, 94.
————, Roman, 95.
Margaret, Anglo-Saxon, Queen of Scotland, 102.
Materials, Proper for Vestments, 68—77, 81, 90.
Matilda, Queen, Gift of, of gorgeous Vestments, 102.
Mellium. See Gremiale, 151.
Mitre, The, 135.
————, Archbishop's, 142.
————, Correct Shape of, 143.
————, Limerick, 140.
————, Of the Pope, from ancient MS., 142.
————, Of St. Thomas of Canterbury, 138.
————, Of William of Wykeham, 137, 140.
Mitres, "After the old fashion," 141.
————, Standing, 140.
Molinet, Extracts from, 125, 144.

Index.

Monastery of St. Blase, Copes at, as illustrated by Gerbert, 103.
Morse, The, 110.
Mount St. Mary's, Wonderful Cope belonging to, 15.
Mozetta, The, 155.
Mundatory, The, 129.

Offertory Veil. See Benediction Veil, 113.
Oliver Cromwell, Destruction of Sacred Works by, 7.
Orarium. See Stole, 86.
Ordo Missæ Pontificalis, Reference to, 14th century, 150.
Ordo Romanus, ——— 12th century, 149.
———————, ——— 13th century, 141.
———————, ——— 14th century, 176.
Orphreys, 49, 59.
————, Ancient Needlework, 14, 107.
————, Cloth of Gold, 73.
————, Satin, 72.
————, Velvet, 72.
————, Woven Lace, 63, 188.

Pænula. See Chasuble, 43.
Pall, The, 129.
Pallium, The, 167.
Papal Choir, Robes of Cardinals of the, 146, 153.
Pectoral, The, 59.
Pellicia. See Surplice.
Percy Shrine, Beauties of the, 7.
Planeta. See Chasuble, 43.
Pontifical, High Mass. See Frontispiece, and 191.
Pope Benedict the Twelfth, Reference to, 122.
—— Boniface the Eighth, ——— 142.
—— Eutychianus, ——— 78.
—— Gregory the Tenth, ——— 141.
—— Innocent the Third, ——— 150.
—— Pius the Ninth, ——— 36, 142, 155, 162, 168, 170, 171.
—— Sylvester, ——— 78.
—— Urban the Fifth, ——— 142.

199

Index.

Powdering for Chasuble, 71.
Psalter of Queen Mary, 65, 122.
Psalter of Richard the Second, 1, 80.
Purificator, The, 129.
Purple, 4.
———, Ancient Imperial, 4.
———, Hermione, 4.
———, Rose, 4.
———, Stoles, 97, 98.
———, Tyrian, 5.

Queen of Spain, costly gift of Tiara, to Pius the Ninth, 142.

Rational, The, 54.
Ravenna, Bishops of, from Mosaics, 48, 167.
———, Diptych Chasuble of, 45.
———, John, Archbishop of, 94.
Rebus, frequent use of, in ancient embroidery, 20.
Red, anciently, a penitential colour, 176.
Revolution, French, effect of, on the usages of the Church, 56.
"Roc." See Tunicle, 83.
Rochet, The, 144.
Roman, Ancient, Vesture, 2, 3, 4, 43, 44, 47, 49.
———, Catacombs, Frescoes of the, 79, 138.
———, Collar, 173.
———, Modern, Vestments, 55, 92, 95, 100, 162, 188.
———, Pall, 129.

Reference to—
St. Agnes, 168.
St. Andrew, 20.
St. Apollinaris, 45.
St. Augustine, 47.
St. Austin, 47.
St. Benedict, 135.
St. Birinus, 149.
St. Cuthbert, 159.

Index.

St. Dunstan, 57.
St. Edward the Confessor, 101, 121, 136.
St. Egino, 160.
St. Genevieve, 139.
St. George, 112.
St. Gregory the Great, 83, 94, 167.
St. Hugh, 102.
St. John the Evangelist, 1, 20, 32, 135.
St. James, 135.
St. Katherine, 105.
St. Livinus, 47.
St. Paul, 27, 41, 43.
St. Peter, 54, 93, 168.
St. Stephen, 80.
St. Thomas of Canterbury, 48, 57, 139.

St. Blase, Monastery of, 103.
St. Frideswide's Monastery, Oxford, 175.
St. George's Cathedral, Southwark, 130, 188.
St. George's Chapel, Windsor, 141.
St. Jean de Chartres, Abbey of, 147.
St. John Lateran's, the Pope's Cathedral, 169.
St. Mary's College, Oscott, 19.
St. Mary Hill, London, 145.
St. Mary Magdalene, Oxford, 157, 161.
St. Paul's, Old, 12, 157, 164.
Sacristan, Duties of the, 186.
Sandals, The, 159.
——————, of Bishop Giffard, 160.
——————, of Bishops of Ravenna, 160.
——————, of Bishop Waneflete, 161.
——————, Correct form of, 161.
——————, Decoration of, 161.
——————, of St. Egino, 160.
——————, of Thomas de la Mare, 160.
Smith, Lord William, Gifts of, to Lincoln Abbey, 32.
Soutane, The, 146, 171.

Index.

Stitches, Anglo-Saxon Embroidery, 177.
———, Early Mediæval Embroidery, 180.
———, Tacking, 76.
Stole, The Sacrificial, 86.
——————————, Correct Materials for, 90.
——————————, Dimensions of, 89.
——————————, Fringe for, 91.
——————————, Making up of, 91.
——————————, Ornamentation of, 90.
Stole, The Baptismal, 97.
————— Confessional, 98.
————— Preaching, 100.
————— Roman, 92.
Stolone, The, 96.
Subcingulum, The, 148.
Succinctorium, The, 150.
Sudarium, The, 93.
Surplice, The, 121.
————— Ancient, 122, 123.
————— Correct, 124.
————— French, 123.
"Swastica." See Gammadion, 139.

"Taisselli," 105.
Tarquin, Purple Tunic presented to, by Etruscans, 5.
Tassels for Dalmatic, 81.
————— Girdle of Alb, 42.
————— Offertory Veil, 115.
————— Prelates' Gloves, 163.
Tau, or **T** Cross, 50.
Thomas de la Mare, The Munificent, 53, 165.
Tiara, The Pope's, 142.
Tintinnabulum, 91.
Titulus of Mitre, 141.
Tunica-linea, 145.
Tunicle, 81, 83.
———, Decoration of, 85.

Index.

Veil, The Chalice, 116.
———— Offertory, 113.
Vestments, Directions for Making, 74.
————, Exaggerated richness in, 71.
————, Figured Silk for, 71.
————, Velvet, 72.
Vestment-maker's Charge to the Sacristan, 186.

Wells Cathedral, Rich Bequests to, 12.
William the Conqueror, Appropriation by, of English Vestments, 22, 105, 150.
Winchester Cathedral, Gift of Cardinal Beaufort to, 13.
Worcester Cathedral, Sandals from Tomb of Bishop Giffard in, 160.

Y, The, Cross, 49, 60.
Yellow Vestments, substituted for Black, 176.

LONDON : PRINTED BY WILLIAM CLOWES AND SONS, STAMFORD STREET
AND CHARING CROSS.

www.ingramcontent.com/pod-product-compliance
Lightning Source LLC
Chambersburg PA
CBHW031346230426
43670CB00006B/446